ENJOY PRAYING

by

MICHAEL AND TERRI QUINN

FAMILY CARING TRUST

First published 1991
by Family Caring Trust
44 Rathfriland Road
Newry
Co. Down
BT34 1LD
Tel Newry 64174

Copyright © Family Caring Trust, 1991
ISBN 1 872253 04 0

Illustrations and design: Pauline McGrath
Typesetting: Cassidy Printers, Newry
Printing: Universities Press (Belfast)

Bible text is reproduced from the
Good News Bible © American Bible Society,
New York, 1966, 1971 and 4th edition 1976,
published by the Bible Societies/
Harper Harper Collins, with permission.

Reprinted 1994

DEDICATION

TO PETER DEVLIN, WHO PRAYED WITH US, TAUGHT US ABOUT PRAYER,
AND LED US TO OTHERS WHO PRAYED.

CONTENTS

INTRODUCTION

This is quite a simple book. It is aimed at anyone, young or old, who wants to learn to pray, to grow in friendship with God — and also to improve the quality of their life, including their family life and their other relationships. Parents, teenagers, single adults, grandparents... Anyone who wants to gain a sense of what is important — and the energy to go on loving amid the pressures and conflicts of day-to-day living. It is to help you discover how enjoyable prayer can be and enable you to experience the benefits of prayer in your daily life.

This book has been used by some people as an **introduction** to prayer, but people who have experienced other courses on prayer, or who are more advanced in prayer have also found it useful.

The bible is different

The aim of the book is to support you as you learn and practise simple methods of praying with the gospels. There are many other forms of prayer and meditation, including methods from your own faith tradition, which are not included here, and which you will naturally continue to use. There are also many beautiful formal prayers which may be more suitable than the Bible at times — sometimes we **need** formal structured prayers. But the Bible is special. It is the main source of prayer for Christians.

At the end of each chapter there are suggested passages for prayer in the week ahead. These are taken from the New Testament, because people usually find New Testament stories easier to begin with, (and because the Old Testament tends to make more sense to people who are familiar with the New).

Which version?

Feel free to use whatever version of the New Testament appeals to you — preferably one with the text divided into short sections with headings, as in the Good News or Jerusalem versions. The quotations in this book are taken from the Good News Bible, because it is acceptable to most Christian denominations, and because its language is simple.

Part of a course

The book is designed to be useful on its own, as part of a do-it-yourself course, but it is particularly effective as part of a six-week course in a small group of up to ten people. Perhaps that needs to be borne in mind, for this is not a book to be read in one go; it is best read one chapter at a time, and used as a workbook. The leader's guide for the course is available separately from Family Caring Trust.

Prayer is communication with God — not a method. Methods of prayer should only be used in so far as they are helpful, for we all have different personalities. A number of different methods are introduced in this book, therefore, and you are encouraged to try them out a number of times in order to find out what **does** suit you.

A note on language

God is obviously neither male nor female, but unfortunately our language has never developed a way of coping with that. So the fact that we occasionally refer to God as 'he' has no special significance.

Acknowledgements

None of the methods of praying in this book is original; they are all methods that have stood the test of time, and which the authors have learnt from others. The books mentioned in the recommended reading list at the back have been especially influential.

We should like to acknowledge our debt to the following people who read and commented on the book in its draft form, or who tested it out with groups of people from a variety of religious and social backgrounds: Gabrielle Allman, Michael Bannon, Brenda Blaney, Vernon Blyth, Carmel Clark, Ray Davey, Peter Devlin, Vera Durkin, Stephen Ferris, David Gamble, Andrew Graystone, Finbarr Lynch, Karen Martyniuk, Brendan McAllister, Catherine and Michael Molloy, Charles O'Connor, Joan and Malcolm Scott, Brian Smeaton — also our children, Fiona and Ciaran, and our always willing secretary, Bernie Magill.

CHAPTER ONE: PREPARING TO MEET GOD

Sue and Keith go to great lengths to prepare for a date. They think about each other a lot during the day, picturing each other, wondering what the other is doing, remembering things to tell each other. As the time to meet approaches, there can be no doubt as to what is uppermost in their thoughts. Keith combs his hair this way and back that way, he puts on his best clothes, polishes his shoes, combs his hair once again — usually in yet another way — and even plans what he will talk about to keep the conversation alive and interesting. Sue tries on different dresses, skirts, blouses, wanting to look her very best for Keith. And she is filled with excitement as the time approaches..

Looking forward

It is obvious that they love each other. The preparations they make show that — but the interesting thing is that these very preparations are also a way of making their love grow.

Think for a moment about the opposite situation — for example when you meet someone you love who seems to be more taken up with work than with you, who seems scarcely even to have thought of you since the last time you met. That cools your love a little, doesn't it? Whereas it tends to make such a difference when you meet someone who is interested in you, who has thought about you, and who looks forward to being with you. Your love can grow.

Isn't it the same with meeting God in prayer. How can you expect suddenly to switch on if you have not prepared, if you have not thought, if you have not looked forward? For prayer is not just some kind of mental exercise — it is a meeting with a loving friend, and many of the things you do to develop a human friendship apply also to your friendship with God. It is not surprising that some people find prayer difficult and boring until they begin to spend time preparing and looking forward to meeting this friend.

Meeting with God in scripture

Long before they are due to meet again, people in love think about each other and look forward to meeting. It is the same with prayer; many people choose some verses from the Bible beforehand and even read them at bedtime on the previous evening. You may like to try that with the passages suggested at the end of each chapter.

You are not, of course, meeting a **passage** in prayer; you are meeting **God**. You may wonder how a passage from the Bible can help you to meet God. But the Bible is no ordinary book. It

those very preparations are a way of making their love grow

is a very special book. As you read it, God is really and truly present. **The events and experiences of two thousand years ago come to life as you read a passage of the New Testament. Jesus is present. What he does and says can now be done and said directly to you.** You are no longer 'reading a passage', even praying about a passage; you are meeting a person; you are listening and talking to Jesus. That is why it makes so much sense to prepare.

Creating the right atmosphere

Part of preparation is making the switch from the pressures of daily living and creating an atmosphere that brings us into the peaceful presence of God. There are various things which people find useful in helping them to do this.

One obvious help is to decide on a time and place that is free from distractions. You may have to experiment a bit until you find what time suits you best. Are you freshest early in the morning or later in the evening? Consider getting up a little earlier in the morning to pray — many people claim their whole day is different as a result of that start. But don't leave it to chance — if you decide prayer is important to you, you will probably not be happy to leave it until last thing before bedtime, when you may be too tired to think. Having a regular time can be a great help.

Where you pray will also affect how you pray. Most people seem to prefer to pray in a quiet room at home, often in a special 'sacred' corner of the room where the Bible, and possibly a cross, are kept. But there are some who find the peace they need at the back of a church or in a park or on a country walk — even in the bath! See what suits you.

Everything ready

Looking for a passage in your Bible can be a great time-waster. It helps to mark the correct place before you start. Some like to light a candle before the open book as a reminder of the presence of Christ, the light of the world — and of the prayer of the Holy Spirit that is already going on within us. Why not? Remember the pains people in love take to set the right atmosphere for a meal by arranging flowers, lighting a candle on the table, and choosing the right record or tape. In the same way, some people find that instrumental music, played softly in the background, creates just the right atmosphere for beginning to pray (though some people find music irritating and therefore should not use it).

Another help is to have a notebook and pen or pencil beside your Bible before you start. This has two purposes. Firstly, you may need to jot down some things that occur to you, like 'Post letter' or 'Pay milkman' rather than let these things return to distract you during your prayer. Secondly, many people recommend that you take a minute or so to write briefly about your prayer when you have finished — how it went, how you felt, whether you met God, whether you were real, what stood out for you or surprised you. This writing can be a great help to growing and improving in prayer.

But there are so many pressures today..

'But we all live such a rushed life today, with so many distractions and so many pressures,' many people complain, 'I find it really hard to switch off from job and family to try to become aware of the presence of God!'

That is a real difficulty. And that is why it is helpful to take a few minutes to relax at the beginning of prayer. A few minutes of stillness to slow yourself down, relax and breathe more slowly and easily, and reduce your heart-rate. In that way, you can also begin to pray **with** your body as well as with your heart and mind.

Some people can be like the little girl who heard that oranges were tasty and bit right into

one. It tasted bitter because she had not peeled off the outer skin. Trying to enter directly into prayer can be frustrating if you have not taken the time to shed the outer layers of busy-ness and pressure in order to enter into your inner self. But how do you do this?

It is usually helpful, whether you sit, kneel or squat cross-legged, to keep your back straight while praying. Otherwise, you may become too comfortable and fall asleep! It may also help to **change** posture for different sections of your prayer, as suggested below — that should keep you more awake and aware, if nothing else. Apart from that, though, make yourself comfortable, and try taking slow, deep breaths, perhaps for two or three minutes. (If you are very tense, you might try tensing and then relaxing all your muscles, starting with your feet and moving gradually up to your head). As you breathe in slowly, you may like to repeat over and over a prayer like 'Come Holy Spirit' or 'Lord, teach us to pray' or 'Our Father', or the name 'Jesus'. But there are many possibilities — the early part of 'Sadhana' by Anthony de Mello (see recommended reading) offers lots of tried and tested methods of quietening down and entering into prayer. These methods can help you 'centre down' and prepare for prayer — and they gradually become part of the prayer. After a few minutes of quiet you should be in a different mood, readier for meeting God.

Becoming aware of God

God is within you, already present, loving you dearly. You may now like to become more fully aware of that presence — rather than go straight

in a quiet room at home . . .

into talking about yourself and your worries. Isn't it a strange way to treat a friend if you are always so anxious to get down to talking about yourself that you do not even take time to become aware of who it is you are talking to!

But how do you become aware of God's presence? Teresa of Avila, a woman who had a deep experience of meeting Jesus in prayer, recommends that you begin your prayer by **'noticing God noticing you.'** Become aware, for example, of Jesus looking at you with love. If you find it difficult to imagine Jesus smiling at you, (as some people do), you might try listening to him as he tells you how he loves you just as you are, or picture him coming into the room, sitting beside you and taking your hand — or just sense the presence of God — whatever helps. Another way to become aware of God's presence is to look at a cross or icon or picture that helps you to 'notice God noticing you'. Use illustrations from this book, if they help. or find a picture that helps you, (for example in Joyce Huggett's book 'Open to God' — you may want to cut a few of the pictures out of it and frame them for use in your place of prayer).

Open to God's word

Your awareness of God's presence may be all you need to spark off prayer. If so, stay in that loving presence for as long as you like. There is no need to move on further. But once you are ready to move on, you may like to respond to God's love by kneeling down or raising your hands as you make an offering of yourself in return and open yourself up to the Spirit. At the same time, ask the Holy Spirit to teach you to pray — perhaps something like "Dear Lord, I

have come to get to know and love you more and to follow you more closely. I haven't come to ask you to do my will, but to open myself to what you want for me. I offer myself and my prayer to you. Please guide me, and teach me to pray."

That is a good frame of mind with which to go into prayer. It is neatly summed up in the words of the musical 'Godspel' — to "see you more clearly, love you more dearly, and follow you more nearly." You are ready now, open to God's word as you read the gospel story slowly and attentively, perhaps in a low voice, believing that what you read is meant for you personally here and now (allowing, of course, for differences of culture and circumstances!) Look for Jesus as you read, and pick out a word or phrase that strikes you. Stay with that word or phrase, repeat it again and again until it sinks into your heart, and pray about how it applies to you. Then move on to another phrase.

Prayer, like life itself, is meant to be enjoyed. But there may also be times when you will feel **intense** joy, or see bright lights, or experience tingling feelings, or shed tears... These experiences should never be taken as a sign of progress in prayer — they may not even be from God. So never judge your prayer. There may be other times when you will not feel any consolation or warmth. Your entire prayer may feel empty and dry. You may be distracted and bored. But don't judge that prayer either — an effort to pray is already prayer. Your very dryness may be the test of how sincere your love is. You may **feel** no love, but your willingness to set time aside in spite of these difficulties may be far more pleasing to God than prayer which

. . . or in the park . . .

. . . or finding peace at the back of a church

is full of sweetness and warmth. Indeed, it is good to decide in advance how long you will pray for, and to stay praying for that time even if you are struggling or feel dry — and not to exceed that time even if you are enjoying your prayer intensely. People following this course might try praying for fifteen minutes each day.

Summing up

In this first chapter we have taken time to look at how to prepare for prayer. The emphasis, as in all the other chapters, has been on meeting a friend. This is central. In future chapters we will be looking at different methods of prayer, different ways of communicating that enable our friendship with God to deepen and our love to grow. You will not find every method right for you. By exploring different approaches, however, you can discover and practise ways of communicating with this friend that suit you and that help you to grow in **accepting** God's love. This should also help you to respond with love to God, to your family, and to everyone you meet.

SOME TIPS FROM CHAPTER ONE

1 MARK YOUR BIBLE
Mark the correct place in your Bible before you start — even read it once at bedtime the night before.

2 DECIDE ON A SUITABLE TIME
Don't leave it to chance — decide in advance on a time when you are normally alert.

3 FIND A PLACE THAT SUITS YOU
A quiet room or space, on a train, at the back of a church — even out walking, if that helps you to pray.

4 HAVE A NOTEBOOK AND PEN TO HAND
To write briefly about your prayer afterwards, and possibly to jot down distractions.

5 KEEP YOUR BACK STRAIGHT
Whether you sit, kneel or squat cross-legged, try to keep your back straight.

6 CENTRE DOWN

Take a short time to quieten down, to relax your body and breathe more slowly and evenly — so that you will be praying with your body as well as with your mind.

7 BECOME AWARE OF GOD'S PRESENCE

'Notice God noticing you'. Picture Jesus sitting with you, look at a picture, or whatever you find helps you.

8 ASK THE HOLY SPIRIT TO TEACH YOU TO PRAY

Respond to God's presence by kneeling or raising your hands as you offer yourself and your prayer. Open yourself to the Spirit. Something like: "Dear Lord, I have come to get to know and love you more and to follow you more closely. I haven't come to ask you to do my will, but to open myself to what you want for me. I offer myself and my prayer to you. Please guide me, and teach me to pray."

9 READ SLOWLY

Take your time. It often helps to read a Bible passage in a low voice, as if the words were addressed to you. Allow time for the words to sink in. Stay with any word or phrase that strikes you, turn it over in your mind, repeat it again and again, and pray about how it applies to you. Then move on to another phrase.

SOME OF YOUR COMMENTS

The 'Comments' section at the end of each chapter is made up of comments made by people who experienced the six-week course associated with this book.

This is a new way of praying for me, but I need a new way. I'm not happy any longer with rhyming off prayers.

It's hard to get used to the idea that this is prayer. I've always seen the Bible as something you **read**, not something you pray with.

I have never been able to get up early in the morning, because I always felt so sleepy, so I didn't even consider praying with Scripture in the mornings. But eventually I realised that I was too distracted and exhausted after work in the evenings. I love getting up to pray now, and I find it a great fresh start to my day.

I prefer this type of prayer because of the atmosphere. The relaxation time helps you to settle and think things over, and the music also adds to the prayer.

My best time for prayer is on Thursday afternoons when I have the house to myself. I can't describe the difference it makes to know I'll have no distractions or interruptions. You need that. Other days, it's really hard to get fifteen minutes.

It's nice to have the passages decided for you so that you don't have to go hunting in the Bible for something to pray on. I like the lists of selected readings and the ideas on how to use them, the fresh ideas on old passages.

The Tips are very useful. And it's a change to have someone leading me in prayer so I just have to listen.

I couldn't believe it when they started to play music and asked us to relax with breathing exercises. I thought 'What has this to do with prayer, or how did I get in with this crowd!'

What I think I'm gaining most is the way I'm learning to link the gospels to my everyday life.

I found that when I talked to God as a friend rather than someone distant from me, prayer was easier.

A GOSPEL STORY TO PRAY ON

After reading the following story, close your eyes and imagine what the upper room was like. See the disciples — what they are wearing, their faces.. Be there yourself in the room with them. Jesus enters. Let him speak the words to you.. This is not just imagining. Jesus is really present.

John 20 19-21 Jesus appears to his disciples.
It was late that Sunday evening, and the disciples were gathered together behind locked doors, because they were afraid of the Jewish authorities. Then Jesus came and stood among them. 'Peace be with you,' he said. After saying this, he showed them his hands and his side. The disciples were filled with joy at seeing the Lord. Jesus said to them again, 'Peace be with you.'

PASSAGES FOR PRAYER DURING THE NEXT WEEK
— ON GOD'S LOVE FOR US

Take time this week to pray for a deep sense of thankfulness and to become aware of the many ways in which God has loved you. Read one of the following passages just before you go to bed. Next day, read it when you begin to pray, applying it to yourself. Don't just **think** about the passage. Pause over any word or phrase that strikes you, talk to God in your own words (or without words), and listen in your heart to what God is saying to you through the passage. Stay with a phrase as long as you need to, even for the whole prayer — or for a few days. Move on to another phrase when you feel you are ready.

There are some suggestions as to how you might pray with each passage, but **they are only suggestions**. Pray in your own way.

Remember to take a few minutes to keep a record in a notebook of how your prayer went. Not so much your thoughts or insights as your feelings and what happened for you. Was prayer dry or consoling, for example? Were you able to use your imagination? Did you meet God? Were you real? What stood out for you or surprised you? Your writing can be a great help to growing and improving in prayer.

JOHN 20 19-21 **Jesus appears to his disciples**. You may like to return to this passage, to enter the upper room and meet the risen Jesus again. Let him repeat to you a number of times 'Peace be with you' What is preventing you from letting his peace into your heart?

MARK 6 30-32 **Come away for a while and rest**. Jesus is not just concerned about the twelve. He is concerned about you. Let him tell you how much he wants you to find peace. Talk to him about how you feel as you start this course or 'retreat,' tell him what your needs are, and what you hope to gain. If you feel this passage is too short, you might continue reading from Mark about the feeding of five thousand — another sign of how generous God wants to be with us.

LUKE 12 22-32 **No need to fear, for your Father loves you**. This does not mean that you will not **feel** fearful at times. Talk about your fears. You could repeat any phrase or word that strikes you until it begins to sink into your heart.

JOHN 3 16-17 **How much God loves you**. If you find this hard to believe, say so. Talk to God about it. But trust also in his love, and be grateful. See how one word or phrase takes on new meaning as you slowly repeat it over and over.

MATTHEW 7 7-11 **How much more will your Father in heaven give you good things**. You might picture Jesus saying these words — can you see the look in his eyes? Ask him what the Father wants to give you...

1 CORINTHIANS 13 1-13 **God is love**. You could try substituting the word 'God' for 'love' as you read, and see what the passage means to you. Repeat over and over a phrase that strikes you, and talk to God about it.

EPHESIANS 1 1-14 **Spiritual blessings in Christ**. What word or phrase strikes you as you read? Try repeating it slowly, again and again, letting it sink in.

Because this is an introduction to prayer, the emphasis is on the New Testament, but there are many beautiful passages in the Old Testament about God's love for us. You might like to try PSALM 139 1-18 or ISAIAH 43 1-5 AND 49 14-16. Again, pick a phrase, repeat it, pray about it, let it sink in...

PLANNING

During the next week, experiment to find what time of the day might suit you best for prayer. Can you pray after a meal, or do you feel too sleepy? When do you normally feel too tense — or too exhausted. When are you freshest? Try getting up a little earlier in the morning — you may have to put the alarm out of reach so that you have to get out of bed to switch it off!

This week I will try praying at the following times...

_____

_____

CHAPTER TWO: THE JESUS WE MEET

The wrong picture

Christine prays regularly, but she feels a great deal of guilt and 'duty' in her approach to God. Indeed, it is difficult for her to put a face on the God she prays to because she finds it so hard to imagine a smiling, encouraging Jesus. She has always been a little frightened of Jesus.

Sadly, she is not alone in that, for many people are handicapped in their approach to God by a distorted picture of the very person whom God sent to help us know him. For them, Jesus often comes across as a judging and demanding figure. This is not altogether surprising. For this is the image of Jesus presented in some well-intentioned sermons, books and pictures. Many people pray today with pictures from the Eastern Church called icons, and it is good that these icons are now coming into their own, but in some of them Jesus looks extremely severe — perhaps even frightening.

That can be a pity. In this course on prayer we are encouraging people to pray regularly. But what is the point in us praying more if the Jesus we are praying to is a judge watching out for and recording all our mistakes, and constantly pointing an accusing finger of guilt at us? Compare it to a human relationship. If you have to talk with someone you see as very removed or distant or cross — for example, if you go to have a chat with the boss at work, or whoever might be a boss figure in your life — you're probably going to feel cautious and awkward, even fearful. Isn't it the same with Jesus?

The real Jesus

So who is Jesus for you? Is he someone to whom you can say 'I love you' but find it hard to say 'I like you?' Is he someone who is generally displeased with you, disappointed with you? If so, you need to pray for a true picture of an understanding friend who is far more delighted with you than you can imagine. It may come as a surprise that he is asking you, not so much to love him as to let him love you! You do not have to do anything, or be loving, before he loves you. He is what your heart was made for. It is **essential** to clear away any false images and get to know this person as he really is. For that is surely the best reason for going to prayer — to meet Jesus, to discover him as the best of all possible friends, to grow in love with him, and to learn to follow him. How can you follow and imitate someone whom you misunderstand and are not drawn to? Moreover, Jesus himself said that you cannot know the Father if you don't know him.

How do you meet this Jesus? A great way to meet him is in the New Testament. There you find the true icon or picture. We saw in the last chapter that the Bible is no ordinary book. No history book, no life story, no novel, was ever like this. For Jesus is **present** when you read the New Testament. He is there for you to meet. If you have ever regretted not being alive in the time of Jesus, you won't believe what can happen when the Holy Spirit opens your eyes and you meet Jesus in the gospels, when you listen and look and move up close to speak with him. The person you meet there is a far more human, compassionate, good-humoured, encouraging, interested friend than you might expect!

Jesus the encourager

Can you think of someone you have met at any time during your life whom you loved and really wanted to be like? Someone who liked you a lot, who put you at ease, was warm, maybe teased you gently. Someone with an attractive inner peace and calm. Someone who made you feel good about yourself. Someone whose smile and caring and humour and presence inspired you and made you want to be more like him or her. Well, that person is perhaps the nearest you can come at present to appreciating the person of Jesus. But (s)he is still only a pale shadow of the most wonderful person who ever walked the earth.

I suppose the first thing you notice about Jesus is that he is **the great encourager**. His smile and his touch, his warmth and caring are all part of his healing, part of what draws people to follow him and makes them want to be his disciples. They feel respected by him, even by the way he asks questions and encourages them to think and talk for themselves. People feel loved, appreciated, good about themselves, healed, whole — in fact, his whole message is one of hope and encouragement and freedom, not just for the future but right here and now in this life as well.

Jesus the friend

Look at him having a meal. He chooses to eat with all sorts of people, especially the downtrodden, the disadvantaged and the misfits of society. People who are disliked — whom nobody encourages. Prostitutes. Well-known sinners. People like the tax-collectors who are hated and who hate themselves for collecting taxes for the Romans. All this at a time when having a meal with someone is like saying 'You are my special friend.' That upsets many people, but Jesus loves these poor, neglected 'sheep without a shepherd' and feels for them so deeply that he doesn't care what others think of him.

What do you think the atmosphere was like at the table, and what do you imagine they talked about? In limited space, the gospels only hint at the details, so it can help to fill in the details ourselves. We tend to put so much emphasis on Jesus being God that we can assume he spent his time talking about God and religion. That is not very likely. Don't forget that he was human. You can be quite sure these people chatted about local events, fishing catches, and crops, and that they told stories and joked and laughed and sang songs. Jesus himself said there was a time to weep and a time to laugh, a time for fasting and a time to celebrate. His first miracle provided an enormous quantity of wine for celebrating the wedding at Cana. He knew how to celebrate, to sing and to tease (can you imagine the laughter and teasing among the disciples when he gave James and John the nickname 'Sons of Thunder!') and to laugh until the tears came to his eyes at some of the funny stories told around the table. Otherwise, why do you think his

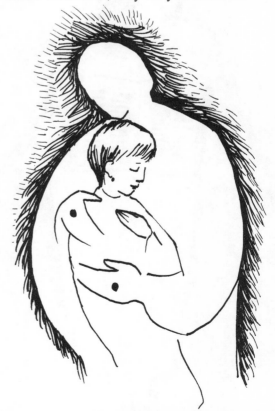

It may come as a surprise that he is asking you, not so much to love him as to let him love you.

company was so attractive, or why were these tough, hardened people so delighted to dine with him! And why were the Pharisees so annoyed at this merry 'wine-drinker!' No, the atmosphere at those meals was marvellous. But can you imagine that? Or is your Jesus too much 'God' to allow him to be human — to scratch himself, to take time off to put his feet up and relax with friends, to cry bitter tears, or to hold his sides with laughter!

look at him having a meal

The compassionate Jesus

Look at the final meal with his disciples (John 21). This is a more serious occasion, of course, but Jesus is in a delightfully playful mood. He has planned a surprise for his friends. He has lit a fire and is grilling fish for them, but he can't resist a final tease — the kind of thing we might do for a prank. In disguise, he shouts to them in their boat and asks if they have caught any fish (though he knows they haven't). So he tells them to try starboard. A huge catch follows — his playful way of saying 'Guess who's here!' When they do arrive, he even teases them by telling them 'Bring some of **your** fish' — as if poking fun at the fact that he had caught the fish for them himself. The whole scene, of course,

For Jesus is present when you read the New Testament

throws great light on the sensitivity of Jesus — poor Peter was finding it so hard to forgive himself for denying Jesus, and this was a beautifully sensitive way to set the right atmosphere for a meal at which they would be reconciled.

This sensitivity to people is one of the loveliest things about Jesus. He wept with Martha and Mary for their brother Lazarus. The gospels are full of examples of his **compassion for those who are suffering, weak, discouraged or needy — he carries them around with him in his heart and reminds them that he has come to take on their burdens**. 'Of course I want to heal you' is his immediate reply to the leper (Mark 1 41, JB), as if anything else is unimaginable. Indeed, it is only because his heart is so full of compassion for the needy, the weak and the poor that he has such hard words for those who oppress his 'little ones.'

He had great warmth, too, with a powerful sense of touch — mentioned again and again in the gospels. Can you just imagine the scene when his disciples came back after being sent out two by two! The smiles and hugging and the delight of being together again. We read about Jesus being betrayed with a kiss, yet we can overlook the fact that such signs of affection were obviously quite normal for him.

Offputting statements?

But was there not another side to Jesus, too? Some people can accept his strong stand against the Pharisees and those who lorded it over the poor; however, they sense a certain lack of humanity, a coldness and distance, in the man who dismisses his mother's arrival with the question 'Who is my mother?' But part of the reason why we are blind to the humanity and sensitivity of Jesus is that his statements are often taken out of context. Look at the scene. Remember first of all that his family have come to take him away, thinking that they know what is in his best interests — "They set out to take charge of him, because people were saying 'He's gone mad!' " (Mark 4 21). He needed to make

You are my family

a statement about that. Remember, too, that, having asked 'Who is my mother?' he then came out with one of the most marvellously encouraging statements ever made. He turned to the poor, simple people he was with, some of them people whom no one had ever believed in, and he told them that **they** were his family. Indeed, all who open themselves up to the Father's Will are included in this gift. So far from being a slight to his mother or family, here was a love without limits — typical of this extraordinarily generous man.

Jesus the challenger

But is his message itself not a very extreme one that can fill us with guilt and give us a sense of never being able to measure up? Does he not expect us to sell all we have and give the money to the poor? Again, the problem is in seeing things out of context. We are not being asked to sell all we have any more than to turn the other cheek, or cut off an arm, or pluck out an eye — that is a manner of speaking to shock us into hearing an important underlying truth. We are being invited, like the rich young man, to look at what is preventing us from following Jesus, what we are over-attached to. In the case of the young man it is wealth; in my case it may be my own way of doing things, my laziness, or my sarcasm... And don't overlook the fact that Jesus 'looked straight at him with love' — and gave him the freedom to choose. The Gospel does not say that the young man would not be saved, but that it would be difficult for him to enter into the Kingdom as long as he remained so deeply attached to material possessions. And Jesus closes this scene by reminding us that even what appears impossible to us is possible with God.

The greatest challenge

So there is a serious and challenging side to Jesus too. Sadly, that is often overlooked today. Other images of Jesus can be as unbalanced as the angry, demanding one. In some pictures and presentations, and in some popular devotions, the real Jesus is even more disguised by layers of make-up, and he comes across as a harmless, sentimental, sad, 'pious', almost plastic Jesus — honoured by us, perhaps, but leaving us in control; not the true God of surprises who can never be neatly packaged and controlled. There is, in fact, a deeply challenging side to Jesus.

But what is the greatest challenge? Isn't it the person of Jesus even more than his teaching? Isn't it his freshness of approach, the freedom within him to respond to needs in new ways? Isn't it the way he lived, the way he sought out the outcasts and the poor — how he cared for them and let his heart be broken, how he spent himself loving them, touching them, encouraging them and healing them? Isn't the real challenge his invitation to follow him and, with his help, assist in the work of healing and transforming human lives?

Jesus 'looked straight at him with love'

SOME TIPS FROM CHAPTER TWO

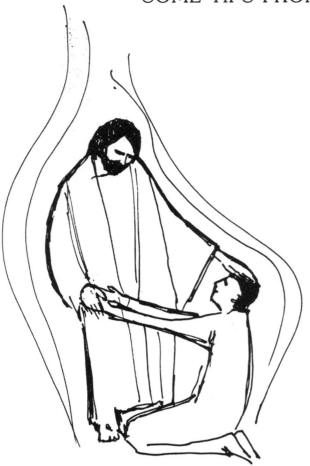

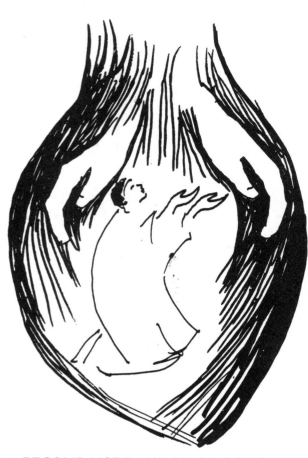

● A TRUER PICTURE OF JESUS

Pray for a true understanding of Jesus as a warm, generous friend. That is a marvellous grace, and one which your Father very much wants to give you. There can hardly be a better way to form this picture than by reading the Gospels and praying on them.

● BECOME MORE AWARE OF GOD'S LOVE

In chapter one, there was a suggestion that you begin prayer by seeing God looking at you with love, by listening to Jesus telling you how he loves you, or by picturing him touching you or sitting with you. Regular practice of this at the beginning of prayer will gradually improve your picture of God — and incidentally of yourself.

● LOOK FOR THE PERSON

The emphasis in prayer, and in reading the gospels, needs to be even more on getting to know and love Jesus than on getting to know his teaching. As you read the Bible, try not to concentrate so much on the 'message' that you miss the person. As you get to know Jesus, you will hear his message with different ears, for you will be aware, for example, of his love of the Father and his compassion, out of which even his harshest words flow.

SOME OF YOUR COMMENTS

When I was small, someone told me that an angel wrote down everything I did wrong and I would have to answer for it after my death. I didn't realise until recently how much harm that picture did. It turned God into a fault-finding judge, and I still find it hard to believe that God is very fond of me.

For me Jesus is now more real as a person. The chapter opened my eyes.

My way of looking at the Scriptures was very limited. I looked for the message. I thought the story of the Good Samaritan was to teach me about doing good for others. I missed the point that Jesus also felt that compassion for me and has cared for me and healed me. You miss a lot when you don't look for Jesus.

The relaxation exercise was very difficult at the beginning. I actually felt tense from my neck down. When I told my husband, he said 'I'm not surprised. You never relax. You'll have a heart attack unless you find some way of calming down.'

The fifteen minutes are so hard to fit in. Evening time is chaotic in our house, and I'm too exhausted by the time the children are in bed. Last week I tried praying in the car outside the school while waiting to pick up the children, but there were too many distractions. I don't know how I'll get up earlier in the mornings, but it looks like that's the only solution!

I'm glad of the awareness I got of not having to pray from duty, or with a sense of shame and guilt.

I especially like praying around one phrase or word.

I have to go away and think about a passage before I'm ready to pray on it, so I read it and go off and make the bed or do something before I come back to settle down and pray.

A GOSPEL STORY TO PRAY ON

In this week's passage we meet someone whose eyes were opened. He saw Jesus and followed him. Can you imagine what the scene was like? And can you let Jesus open your eyes so that you also see him as he really is? Can you also 'follow Jesus on the road?'

Mark 10 46-52 They came to Jericho, and as Jesus was leaving with his disciples and a large crowd, a blind beggar named Bartimaeus son of Timaeus was sitting by the road. When he heard that it was Jesus of Nazareth, he began to shout, "Jesus! Son of David! Take pity on me!" Many of the people scolded him and told him to be quiet. But he shouted even more loudly. "Son of David, take pity on me!" Jesus stopped and said "Call him." So they called the blind man. "Cheer up!" they said. "Get up, he is calling you." He threw off his cloak, jumped up and came to Jesus. "What do you want me to do for you?" Jesus asked him. "Teacher," the blind man answered, "I want to see again." "Go," Jesus told him, "your faith has made you well," At once he was able to see and followed Jesus on the road.

SOME PASSAGES FOR PRAYER DURING THE NEXT WEEK

You may like to return to the story of blind Bartimaeus (Mark 10 46-52) and stay with it for as long as you wish, even for a few days. Apart from that, for prayer over the next week, start at the beginning of Mark's gospel and try reading the first few chapters as if you had never heard the stories before — as if you were reading them for the first time. Read slowly. Look not so much for the **teaching** of Jesus as for the person himself — look **at** him. Stop whenever you want to, or when anything strikes you, and imagine what the scene must have been like. You could look at Jesus in the scene as if you were an observer in the background. See him in action. Fill in the details for yourself. Then you might move in closer — put yourself into the picture, approach Jesus, and let him speak to you personally. Listen to his words spoken to you: 'The time has come. The Kingdom of God is close at hand. Repent.' (1 15 JB) Ask him how he wants you to repent and turn over a new leaf. Hear him invite you to follow him and become a fisher of people. Ask him how he wants you to follow him. Sit at the table with him. Let him tell you how welcome you are. Let him fill your glass. Listen and talk to him.

Remember to take a few minutes to keep a record in a notebook of how your prayer went. Not so much your thoughts or insights as how you felt and what happened for you. Were you able to use your imagination? Did you meet Jesus? Were you real? What stood out for you or surprised you? This writing can be a great help to growing and improving in prayer.

PLANNING

During the next week, experiment with different places for prayer. The obvious place may not be the best one. Which places offer peace and quiet, with fewer distractions? Only by trying them will you discover what helps you most.

This week I will try praying in the following places

_____

_____

CHAPTER THREE: LOVED AND FORGIVEN

Mrs Grainger had two daughters, Sandra and Elaine. When they were small, they were pretty and cute, and everyone was fond of them. As they got older, and more and more rebellious, they were not so attractive, but their mother was still very patient and understanding and loved them deeply. 'They're just going through a rough patch' she would say, 'Rebelliousness is normal.'

'I don't know why she goes on caring!'

The two daughters were increasingly nasty and hostile to their mother, however, and treated her with gross disrespect. Elaine eventually cut all ties with her and left home.

The neighbours were shocked that Mrs Grainger remained patient and understanding. They shook their heads 'She must be blind' they said, 'I don't know why she goes on caring about them. They don't care a damn about her.'

Mrs Grainger wasn't blind. But she was very sad. She felt heart-broken when she thought about Elaine who had cleared off and had never bothered even to write. 'I wonder where she is?' she would think, 'Or what trouble she's got into?.. I'd love to hear from her... Oh, I'd love to throw my arms around her, even to hear her answer me back in anger and maybe then break down and cry her little heart out the way she used to.'

The poor mother watched every day for the postman. But no letter came, and the loneliness and pain ate into her heart.

'There's so much goodness in Sandra'

But Mrs Grainger's greatest pain was with her eldest daughter, Sandra, who had felt it was her 'duty' to stay at home. Sandra did everything right. She worked ceaselessly, and made sure her mother never could find fault with anything she did — but she worked always with hostility

and an air of silent martyrdom. She prided herself on never saying an angry word — no one could point a finger at her — but her attitude to her mother was full of coldness and indifference. That was what her mother found really hard to take. 'Elaine could be headstrong and blunt,' she thought 'But she never treated me as coldly as this.. And yet, deep down, I know there's so much goodness and generosity in Sandra...'

Mrs Grainger felt lonely and disappointed. But she wasn't a woman who allowed herself to get bitter, or who wasted time on self-pity. She had an extraordinary capacity to forgive, to look for goodness and to go on loving.

Breaking point

Many a time that love was put to the test. Especially the day when, after three years, Elaine returned. The overjoyed mother met a seething Sandra, her eyes full of venom and hate.

'Great!' Sandra said, 'Your little pet of a daughter has come home, but don't kid yourself — **she's** not interested in work. All she wants is someone to sponge on. I want her out of here!'

We all have a limit to our patience. For many parents this might have been a breaking point. So Mrs Grainger's answer was all the more remarkable.

'Sandra,' she said, opening her arms, 'My dear, lovely Sandra. You have been so faithful to stay with me all these years. Thank you for being so good — is it any wonder I'm crazy about you!'

Heart-broken but patient

That is the story of the Prodigal Son (Luke 15 11-32). Sometimes a story loses its power when we become over-familiar with it, so a few details have been changed in order to let you hear it freshly. Jesus came to reveal the Father, and he told this story to teach us about the love of the Father for us. Read the gospel story again for yourself, and try concentrating on the father. See this sad, vulnerable, but extraordinarily forgiving man. What is often overlooked is that he has lost **both** sons. The elder brother has no real relationship with his father at all. For a long time he has done all the right things, but with the wrong attitude — ''All these years I have worked for you like a **slave**.'' he says. Duty has taken the place of love for him (as with many of us!) To make matters worse, the elder brother feels superior to his younger brother, despises him, and refuses even to recognise him as brother — ''this son of yours'' he calls him. Can you begin to imagine how hurtful all that must have been to the father? If one of your children treated you like that, you would probably be so angry. Yet this sad, vulnerable old man replies by opening his hands to his angry son and saying "Everything I have is yours."

The point of it all

Why spend so long on this story, or what is so important about it? Well, in this book you are learning to improve your communication in prayer, so it is important to begin by clearing the blocked lines of communication that weaken prayer and even make it ineffective. It is vital to start by forming a clearer picture of who it is you are communicating with, and who you are yourself. And the extraordinary thing is that one of the best ways of discovering who you are is not by looking at yourself so much as by looking at God.

What do you find? First that you are loved. That is one of the most central and important of all truths in the Bible — that God loves you more deeply than you will ever understand. And secondly, that you are a sinner — a well-meaning person who sometimes lives in a way that is isolated, separate, independent of God. Like the man Jesus talked about who spent his

the prodigal son

life building barns to store his grain but forgetting what life was about — someone who worked hard and did his best, but whose life was going in the wrong direction (Luke 12 13-21).

And that is who you are before God — a loved, forgiven sinner. The emphasis here needs to be more on 'loved,' on God loving you and forgiving you as soon as you repent and turn to him rather than on the word 'sinner.' That is what we mean about keeping the focus on God rather than on yourself. But it **is** also important to recognise yourself as a sinner — as someone who falls far short of what God wants you to be.

Needy People

Some people today react against this notion that we are sinners. They want a spirituality that is rooted in good sound psychology, with a positive thrust that enables them to be more human as they grow closer to God. They are absolutely right to want this, and to reject the overemphasis on sin that crippled so many people with guilt in the past. What we are talking about here is a healthy sense of sin, such as the world-famous psychoanalyst, Dr Karl Menninger, called for in his book, "Whatever became of sin?" In that book, he claims that a sense of sin helps us to admit and face up to our own attitudes and behaviour. It is interesting that, in excellent programmes like that of Alcoholics Anonymous, the very first step is to admit that we are powerless, that this behaviour that is destroying me as a person has me beaten, that I cannot heal myself on my own, and that I need a power greater than myself; I need to open myself to accept the love that has always been waiting for me. This is the attitude of the poor sinner at the back of the temple, "God, take pity on me, a sinner!" (Luke 18 9)

And which of us is not an addict? Alcohol, tobacco, drugs and gambling may be the better known addictions, but there are many, many more. It is now being realised that practically everyone suffers from addictions of one kind or another — to food, sweets, coffee, even religion! Many people are addicted to various kinds of sexual thoughts and behaviours. A great many others are addicted to television. Even more may be addicted to work. And many of us are addicted to impressing people, seeking to be important in the eyes of others. In each case there is the same sad cycle: depression, leading to the craving for another 'fix' — we seek escape in the behaviour that attracts us — but that actually leaves us feeling emptier, more depressed, craving again, seeking again to escape, to shut out our negative feelings — yet always seeking in the wrong direction. For there can never be any fulfilment or meaning or happiness in these directions. St. Augustine summed it up so well, many centuries ago:

"You have made us for yourself, O Lord, and our hearts are restless until they rest in you." The first step on the road to recovery is a deep sense of my addiction, of my inability to heal myself by my own power alone. I need to begin with a sense of my sin, as I turn back towards my Father.

I'm not too bad!

Deep down I may think "Well, I'm not **too** bad. I pray and I make sacrifices and I share my money with poorer people. At least I'm not as bad as **some**. Other people are the **real** sinners."

Isn't that very like the attitude of blind superiority and pride of the prodigal son's older brother — and of the pharisee in the temple who fasted and prayed and gave to the poor, but looked down on the humble sinner at the back of the temple whom God loved dearly (Luke 18:9). It is so easy for 'respectable' people to slip into

the very first step is to admit that we are powerless

this mentality of superiority — which is a much deeper sin. It is the mentality which thinks, "Look at all these people coming to church like sheep. They've no idea what they're doing. They're stuck with their traditional practices. The gospel means so little to them." Instead of saying, "These people are my sisters and brothers, with all their faults. I know my tendency to be superior is a far greater sin. Lord, have pity on me, a sinner, a blind person, an addict, a pharisee..."

Two kinds of sinner

For the gospel passages above bring out that there are two kinds of sinner. There is the humble one who knows she or he is a sinner — Jesus could not resist people who were humble enough to come to him and put their faith in him. But there is also the second kind, the person who may do all the right things and keep all the rules but who has no relationship with the father — who looks down on others and feels superior to them. And the point is that that pride, that superior attitude, cuts off communication with God; Jesus kept pointing to the spirit of evil affecting good respectable people who think they are better but whose sin is actually much greater. In the last chapter, we saw that more prayer is not the answer if we are praying to a God who fills us with fear and guilt. But equally, more prayer is not the answer if we are praying with the pride of the pharisee in the temple. We need a truer, humbler image of ourselves as we come to pray. So it is important to pray for an awareness of the sinful patterns in our lives, and the grace to turn them over to God. And to take heart — Saint Augustine reminds us that God loves us most where we like ourselves least.

Chosen and blessed

Now, all this needs to be balanced. Too much emphasis on our sinfulness shows a lack of trust in God's forgiveness. We need a sense of sin, but we need an even deeper sense of being loved — and of God's great goodness within us. God loves us, and is delighted with us. Each of us is specially chosen and blessed by God. My name is written on God's palm.

Obviously, it would be spiritual pride to take the credit myself for my goodness and virtues, but it is equally wrong to deny them. If I don't believe in the goodness of God within me, I'll be apologising for myself when I meet others, perhaps seeing myself as a nuisance and a burden. How can I have a real friendship with someone if I don't respect myself? In the same way, how can I communicate properly with God if I do not forgive and respect myself?

Summing up

To sum up. We develop a better self-image

and a deeper respect for ourselves when we focus less on ourselves and more on our extraordinarily forgiving father. The important person in the story of the Prodigal Son is the vulnerable old father who has lost both his sons but continues to love and forgive. We do well in prayer to focus on him, on how our sin has hurt him, and how he keeps opening his arms, forgiving, saying "Everything I have is yours". Look at him as you pray. None of us wants to cause that kind of hurt. We just had not realised how hurtful our superiority could be, or the damage it could do. Go to him with humility — poor, weak, needy, sinful, but loved — admit your sinfulness, your pride, your rejection of your brothers and sisters, and let him forgive you as he forgives everyone who turns to him, repentant.

Pray that you may see more clearly who you are before God — a forgiven sinner. That is why "Lord Jesus Christ, Son of God, have mercy on me, a sinner" is such a perfect prayer. It is clear from the gospels that we are very specially blessed when we become like little children and go to Jesus, trusting, needy, poor...

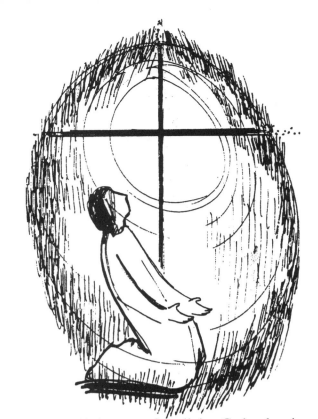

Lord Jesus Christ, son of the living God, take pity on me, a sinner . . .

SOME TIPS FROM CHAPTER THREE

● A TRUER PICTURE OF THE FATHER

Jesus came to us to reveal the Father. That is something he longs to do. Pray to him for a true understanding of the Father as a loving, forgiving friend who is delighted with you. (If your experience of a male figure has been painful, you may find a mother figure more helpful). Refuse to listen to false notions — like the policeman in the sky with a notebook to record all your misdeeds! God made you and loves you and is more patient and forgiving than you can ever imagine.

● A TRUER PICTURE OF YOURSELF

Pray also for a true understanding of who you are before God. A lovable person with many God-given talents and virtues. How can you have a good relationship with someone if you see yourself as a nuisance or burden, if you don't respect yourself? You are a sinner, of course — a well meaning person who sometimes lives life isolated and separate from God — and it is important to pray for a deeper sense of sorrow for the damage these sinful patterns of behaviour do, but you are a **loved, forgiven** sinner, with the emphasis always on the word 'loved,' on **God**, who loves and forgives you, rather than on yourself.

● CONFESS

Your prayer life can be clogged by a lack of repentance — perhaps for sin which you are unwilling to face. It is important to go to God with a repentant heart and confess your sin. This can be a very healing experience.

● AVOID 'NAVEL-GAZING'

Too much looking inwards and self-examination — sometimes called 'navel-gazing' — can do more harm than good. We learn much more about ourselves, and we grow in humility and maturity when we look outwards — to God. Some self-examination may be useful, of course, but the purpose of prayer is to meet God rather than to sort ourselves out. The more we realise how deeply we are loved, the more we will actually tend to appreciate and like ourselves.

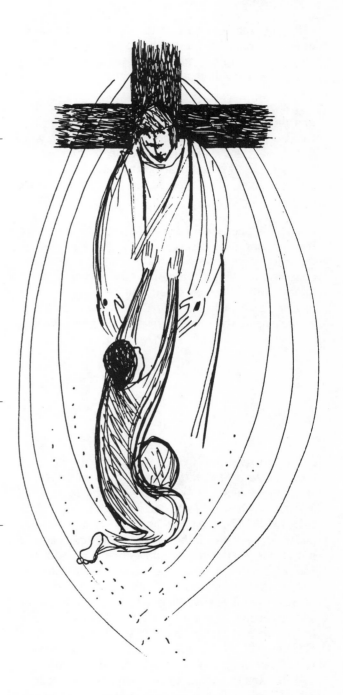

that is who we are before God — loved, forgiven sinners

SOME OF YOUR COMMENTS

I never saw the story of the Prodigal Son like that before. The way I saw it, it was about the sinner instead of about the father. I had always been afraid of God, but this throws a completely different light on him.

For me the best part of the course is the quiet time. It's easier to pray when you relax — though the bright light coming on again is too sudden and spoils it a little for me.

It seems unfair. The older boy worked hard and didn't go off squandering his money on women and drink. But there wasn't much reward for all his hard work. I'd have been annoyed too. I mean, we could all go off and lead reckless lives if we wanted. It's almost as if God prefers sinners.

There's one person I could never forgive. I've tried. I thought I'd forgiven her, but I get all tense again as soon as I see her. And that's what consoled me about the story. God seems to be happy with you even when you're only beginning to make an effort. The son didn't even get saying much of what he had prepared to say.

I really didn't think I was much of a sinner. I was at least a bit better than the average, I thought, and I would never have seen myself superior like one of the pharisees. Now I do see that — and I know I won't change overnight. But at least I know now, and my prayer is 'Lord, take pity on me, a pharisee.'

At the beginning, I saw the quietening time as a chance to relax and take a break — almost to fall asleep for a few minutes. Now I see that it is only by **concentrating** that the real relaxation and preparation for prayer happens.

I felt devastated by the pain of the father. It had never struck me before that he had lost both sons. I had never seen him in that light before — vulnerable and sad. And to think that my arrogant attitude had hurt him like this. I would hate to hurt someone who's already down. But the last straw was when he said 'All I have is yours.' I'd say it was the first time I was ever sorry for my sins because of the way they had hurt someone.

A GOSPEL STORY TO PRAY ON

As you read this week's story, try to concentrate on the father. How does he look? What is he feeling? What does he say to you? What do you want to say to him?

Luke 15 17-32 At last he came to his senses and said, 'All my father's hired workers have more than they can eat, and here I am about to starve! I will get up and go to my father and say, Father, I have sinned against God and against you. I am no longer fit to be called your son; treat me as one of your hired workers.' So he got up and started back to his father. He was still a long way from home when his father saw him; his heart was filled with pity, and he ran, threw his arms round his son, and kissed him. "Father," the son said, "I have sinned against God and against you. I am no longer fit to be called your son." But the father called his servants. "Hurry!" he said. "Bring the best robe and put it on him. Put a ring on his finger and shoes on his feet. Then go and get the prize calf and kill it, and let us celebrate with a feast! For this son of mine was dead, but now he is alive, he was lost, but now he has

been found." And so the feasting began. In the meantime the elder son was out in the field. On his way back, when he came close to the house, he heard the music and dancing. So he called one of the servants and asked him, "What's going on?" "Your brother has come back home," the servant answered, "and your father has killed the prize calf, because he got him back safe and sound." The elder brother was so angry that he would not go into the house, so his father came out and begged him to come in. But he answered his father, "Look, all these years I have worked for you like a slave, and I have never disobeyed your orders. What have you given me? Not even a goat for me to have a feast with my friends! But this son of yours wasted all your property on prostitutes, and when he comes back home, you kill the prize calf for him!" "My son," the father answered, "you are always here with me and everything I have is yours. But we had to celebrate and be happy, because your brother was dead, but now he is alive; he was lost, but now he has been found."

SOME PASSAGES FOR PRAYER DURING THE COMING WEEK

The first four passages below highlight the fact that you are a loved, forgiven sinner. Take time this week to pray for the grace to recognise yourself as a loved sinner. Pray for a deep sorrow for having hurt the vulnerable, forgiving, heart-broken Father who has lost both his sons.

It is suggested that you read the passage for the following day just before you go to bed; then, next day, read it at your prayer time, applying it to yourself. Pause over any word or phrase that strikes you, talk to God in your own words, and listen to what God is saying to you through the passage. Stay with a phrase as long as you need to, even for the whole prayer-time — or for a few days. Move on to another phrase when you feel you are ready.

It is also suggested that on Friday or Saturday you read and pray on one of the passages that will be read in church on Sunday.

Remember to take a few minutes to keep a record in a notebook of how your prayer went. Not so much your thoughts or insights as how you felt and what happened for you. Were you able to use your imagination? Did you meet God? Were you real? What stood out for you or surprised you? This writing can be a great help to growing and improving in prayer.

Luke 15 11-32 **The lost son** — feel free to return to this week's passage, and stay with it as long as you like. Put yourself into the scene and talk with your Father.

Luke 18 9-14 **The Pharisee and the tax collector**. Ask God to help you see how you hurt him by your pride and superiority, and to be able to say, with a deep sense of sorrow, the prayer of the tax-collector. Some people like to slowly with each breath until it sinks deeply into their hearts..

Luke 7 36-50 **The woman who was a sinner**. You might try imagining this scene — it is a wonderful picture of someone with the right attitude, knowing she was a forgiven sinner and responding out of gratitude with tenderness and love. Can you put yourself into the scene?..

Luke 19 1-10 **Zacchaeus**. Think of someone you dislike. Someone you might write off completely. That's the kind of person Zacchaeus was. But see how the God of surprises chooses the least likely — people like you — and makes them so special. And see how generous the forgiven sinner becomes as he turns his life over to God.

Luke 23 32-43 **Jesus is crucified**. See the details as you imagine this scene. See the effects of your sins — and the response of Jesus when you turn to him. Ask him which of your sins hurts him most?

John 8 3-11 **Neither will I condemn you**. These words are spoken to you. It can be so hard to forgive yourself and accept God's pardon — and delight in you. Here is yet more proof of God's constant love and forgiveness.

It is also suggested that you read and pray on some of the passages that will be read in church on Sunday.

PLANNING

During the next week, experiment with different postures for prayer. You need to be comfortable, but not so comfortable that you fall asleep! What about kneeling or standing or lying for **part** of the time? At times, try opening your hands in front of you, or raising your arms. People are often surprised at the effect on their prayer of making a gesture or changing their body posture.

This week I will try...

_____

_____

CHAPTER FOUR: LISTENING WITH THE HEART

I might as well not have been there

'I might as well not have been there. She just wanted to talk and talk about herself, and I couldn't get a word in edgeways. It was awful. At one stage, I thought to myself — this woman doesn't even **see** me, she's totally unaware of me.'

Trapped by a 'talker'

This comment, made recently by a friend, sums up the experience of many people when they feel trapped by someone who is desperate to talk. It can be a frustrating, helpless experience. But do we sometimes do this to God? This example may give a little sense of the imbalance there is when people only want to talk to God but never think of taking time to listen, or to become aware of who it is they are talking to.

The purpose of this course is to learn and to practise better communication methods in prayer — because prayer **is** communication with God. We started by looking at how we can **prepare** better for meeting God in prayer — there were some suggestions on getting down to prayer and preparing to meet God as a friend. Then we looked at how we might develop a truer picture of Jesus and of our Father, and a truer picture of ourselves as both needy and forgiven, because all this is important for clearing the lines of communication. So now we move on to a very important aspect of communication — learning to **listen** better to God in prayer.

A model for listening

The best model we have for listening in prayer is probably Mary. Her faith was rooted, not in miraculous happenings, but in her listening. Apart from the annunciation of the birth of Jesus, the gospels do not record any other

instances when Mary seems to have received a direct message from God. Even there, the most important line in Luke's passage may be "And the angel left her." (Luke 1 38). There was no further information or reassurance. She was left on her own to work out the details. The rest of the messages all seem to have come second hand — from Elizabeth, the shepherds, Simeon, etc. And that's where Mary's listening and faith came in, for Luke tells us a number of times how Mary kept all these things in her heart, treasuring them. It is interesting that Luke uses different words to describe Mary's listening — "treasured", "stored", "pondered"..

So the listening we are talking about is not just listening with our ears, but storing up, pondering, treasuring... How do we listen in this sense? How can we learn to ponder as Mary did, so that, like her, we are overcome by the mysteries of life, and by the sheer wonder and surprisingness of God?

There is no one way to ponder. But there are some methods that have stood the test of time over many years. **Never force yourself with any of these methods, of course — go gently in prayer**. If your prayer gives you a headache, or really disturbs you, there is something wrong. Try a different approach. If one of the following methods does not help you with a passage of Scripture, try another:

Mary kept all these things in her heart . . .

Fishnet listening

One way of learning to listen and to ponder, sometimes called the 'fishnet' method, is to read a gospel passage slowly, pausing when you come to **any word or phrase that strikes you**, and stay with that. After reading a passage, for example, you might ask yourself 'What line or word means most to me in this story?' Come back to that phrase or word, repeat it, perhaps repeat it over and over, and let it sink into your heart. See how the words begin to come alive and affect you. What is Jesus saying to you in all this? What do you think he wants of you? How do you feel? What would you like to say in return? Stay with one word or phrase as long as you need to before moving on.

Let's look at an example. Take the phrase we have already met, 'Lord Jesus Christ, Son of the living God, take pity on me, a sinner.' You might like to repeat that slowly. Or you may prefer to break it into three or four phrases, and to take just one of them at a time for repeating, for storing, pondering, treasuring.. Some people find it helpful to breathe in as they pray the word or phrase — they find themselves opening up to God as they do so — and possibly to breathe out all their stresses and worries and sinfulness with each outbreath.

This same method can be used with set prayers like the Lord's Prayer, taking one phrase at a time — or with a favourite passage of Scripture like 'The Lord is my shepherd.' When you slow down like this with a passage, it is amazing how familiar words take on new meaning. For this is a tried and tested way of listening in prayer — and it is also a method you may like to use when prayer is dry.

Using your imagination

Another method is to use your imagination on scenes from the gospels. Ask yourself what the **scenery** and the **weather** were like, what **sounds** there were, what people were **wearing**, what expressions were on their **faces**, in their **eyes**. Look at Jesus and the people he meets, and hear them speak. Your picture may not be accurate, of course — you may have green fields where there actually were mountains — but that is not important. The point is that looking at the scene in your imagination enables you to think freshly about a passage you may have heard a hundred times, and can suddenly make it come alive for you. You see it differently — and Jesus can become very real for you. Remember that we pray in order to meet Jesus. Here is a marvellous way to meet him and hear him speak to you.

In a previous chapter we saw that it sometimes helps to look at the scene from the outside first, as an observer; then to move in close and meet Jesus, allowing him to do or to say to you what

pausing when you come to any word or phrase that strikes you and staying with it

was done or said in the passage. Or you may prefer to put yourself into the scene right from the start — whichever you prefer. But this is no mere exercise of the imagination. The Holy Spirit is at work as you pray, and the Jesus you meet in the scene is the same Jesus of Nazareth, risen and alive today, bringing to you his peace and healing, and inviting you to be his disciple. It is a great privilege.

The power of questions

Questions offer us another powerful way of listening in prayer. Many a time we read a familiar passage and nothing in particular strikes us. It does not seem to apply to ourselves. At a time like that, it can help a lot to ask questions: 'How does this story apply to me, Jesus? What does it teach me about you? What do you want me to do?'' Ask the Holy Spirit for guidance, and listen in your heart to the answer, to what God wants for you. Perhaps you read a passage in which Jesus is filled with pity for the 'sheep without a shepherd,' and you do not see that as having much to do with your own life — until questions like those above bring out depths of meaning for you. Then you may see that you are one of the hungry sheep needing Jesus yourself — or that you are drifting along with little thought of your own family and their growth in Christ, and that Jesus is now inviting you to think of practical ways of caring for the hungry 'sheep' in your own home.

During the week, many people now read the Scripture passages that will be read in church the following Sunday, and they find that questions like those above help to bring the passages alive for them. This is a practice that is highly recommended, for much Sunday worship is boring precisely because people turn up without preparation, without having reflected, so they see little connection between what is read and what is happening in their lives.

Who asks the questions?

But perhaps an even more important way of using questions is to allow God to ask **you** questions. Again, an example may help. Margaret has a list of people she prays for, her family, neighbours who are ill, friends, an old schoolmate who is going through a rough time with her husband, relatives — a whole list of people in trouble. She also offers herself and all she does each day on behalf of a special area of concern — dying children in countries hit by

. . . a list of the people she wants to pray for . . .

famine, her deceased relatives, peace in various war-torn countries, and so on. For years she has brought her list of requests to God, mentioning the people and things she wants to pray for. There is something very caring and other-centred about this practice, and it is certainly something to be encouraged.

But then, a friend spoke to Margaret about listening in prayer, and what she said had a big effect. Margaret realised that there wasn't much communication with God in bringing along a list of people to prayer. She decided to take a new approach. Next day, she took the first person on her list, her teenage son Mark, and she began to pray **about** Mark instead of **for** him. Praying **about** him meant listening as well as talking. 'What do you want for Mark?' Jesus asked her; and 'Are you sure that is what he most needs?' Then she let Jesus ask her some further questions like 'How do you get on with him?' She had to admit that she had little or no real communication with her son, that they passed like ships in the night most of the time, and that she had never told Mark of her worries about him. 'What worries?' Jesus asked her, and then, 'What's the next step — what do you think you can do about all this?' At the end of ten minutes, she had had a good conversation with Jesus, they had planned to work together on Mark, and she knew Jesus would bless her efforts. She got no further down her list that day, but she could see how real her prayer was — and that this was a far better way to pray for someone than merely to mention them as part of a list.

to use your imagination

A listening heart

These methods are just three ways of listening in prayer: 1. the 'fishnet' method, picking out a word or phrase and letting it sink in; 2. imagining the scene; 3. using questions.

God speaks to us in many ways, of course. Through the events of our daily lives, through nature, through other people, through our bodies, our feelings, our moods.. When we have a headache, a pain in the chest, a feeling of depression, we must not **blame** God, who allows evil — but these can also be messages from a caring Father that there is something wrong with the way we are living, or that we are ready for some change in our lives. Unfortunately, many people ignore these signals and try to cope with bad feelings by taking another beer, another cup of coffee, another tablet. They do not see that God has anything to do with how they are feeling — and they miss so much. God is always waiting patiently, knocking at the door, full of surprises, offering us 'abundant life,' wanting to reveal the Father's will for us.

In this chapter we have looked at ways in which God speaks to us through the gospels. For the Holy Spirit is very active when we read Scripture with a listening heart. Our Father wants us to be open to his Spirit as we read, so that we may get to know and love his son, Jesus, and become his disciples. Each time we open the Bible, extraordinary things can happen when we pray the simple but powerful prayer, 'Come, Holy Spirit' and open ourselves up to the Spirit dwelling in us. There is no way that that prayer will be refused to anyone who is seeking God, who is listening, who has 'ears to hear.'

SOME TIPS FROM CHAPTER FOUR

Here are some ways of listening to God. If one way doesn't help you, try another:

● LET THE WORDS SINK IN

Using the 'fishnet' method, you read slowly, pausing and staying with any word or phrase that strikes you. After reading the passage, come back to that phrase, repeat it, and let it enter your heart, perhaps breathing in the phrase with each breath — like 'Come, Holy Spirit.' See how the words begin to come alive and affect you. Stay on one word or phrase as long as you need to before moving on. This can also be done with set prayers like 'The Lord's Prayer.'

● USE QUESTIONS

Good questions include: 'How does this story apply to me, Jesus? What does it teach me about you? What do you want me to do?' Listen to the answers in your heart. Make time also to listen to the questions God asks **you**: 'Why are you so frightened? What do you need? What do you want for your sister/father/daughter? What can we do together about this?'

● USE YOUR IMAGINATION

Use your imagination to picture the gospel scenes — landscape, weather, clothes, the expressions on faces, in eyes. Look at Jesus and the people he meets, and hear them speak. Remember prayer is to meet Jesus, so look for the **person** even more than for his teaching. Sometimes it helps to look at the scene from the outside first, as an observer; then to move in close and meet Jesus, allowing him to do or say to you what was done or said in the passage. This is not a mere exercise of the imagination. In the gospels you meet the real Jesus of Nazareth, risen and alive today, bringing his peace and healing, inviting you to be his disciple.

SOME OF YOUR COMMENTS

For me, praying was always the same thing as talking. Now I've learned how God can talk back to me.

For prayer I took the passage about the woman who was a sinner and showed such love to Jesus when he was dining at the house of the pharisee. I listened to her talking. 'No one ever believed in me or had any time for me,' she said, 'I was a prostitute, a nobody, I had no belief in myself or respect for myself. But this man didn't condemn me; he believed in me, and looked at me with love. I would do anything for him.' That woman was speaking for me. She helped me to meet Jesus.

What helped me most was picturing the scene from scripture and seeing Jesus as speaking **now** to me.

When I'm tired, I find the 'fishnet' prayer really useful. It makes fewer demands on me to just repeat the same word or phrase, but it keeps my mind focused, and at times it leads to prayer that comes straight from my heart.

I have been made more aware that prayer can be quite simple. I enjoy just talking to God and feeling that he is speaking back. I wish my husband could have done the course with me.

I now listen to the readings on Sunday more closely and try to see what God is saying to me.

Last week, I said I just couldn't ever see Jesus in my imagination, but during the week, I found I could. I saw him clearly walking along the beach, and you know what he was doing? — he was kicking the sand. And when he called the disciples, he used his right arm as well to call them.

Using the first two chapters of Luke, I would ask myself how Mary or one of the others **felt** — their feelings more than their thoughts. That made them more human, and it was more powerful that I could have imagined. I felt very privileged to see and experience Jesus as Mary did.

It was the first time I imagined myself into a Gospel story, and I enjoyed it. It's a new way of praying for me.

I have been listening to God quite a lot, but I didn't realise that was what I was doing.

A GOSPEL STORY TO PRAY ON

For this week's passage, you might imagine the scene, placing yourself among the people on the shore as they listen to Jesus speak from the boat. Some of those who hear him are not listening, not open. You are being invited to be one of the responsive ones, making your heart fertile ground for the Word of God.

Luke 8 5-8,11-15

Once there was a man who went out to sow corn. As he scattered the seed in the field, some of it fell along the path, where it was stepped on and the birds ate it up. Some of it fell on rocky ground and when the plants sprouted, they dried up because the soil had no moisture. Some of the seed fell among thorn bushes which grew up with the plants and choked them. And some seeds fell in good soil; the plants grew and produced corn a hundred grains each. And Jesus concluded, "Listen, then, if you have ears!"

This is what the parable means; the seed is the word of God. The seeds that fell along the path stand for those who hear, but the Devil comes and takes the message away from their hearts in order to keep them from believing and being saved. The seeds that fell on rocky ground stand for those who hear the message and receive it gladly. But it does not sink deep into them, they believe only for a while but when the time of testing comes, they fall away. The seeds that fell among thorn bushes stand for those who hear, but the worries and riches and pleasures of this life crowd in and choke them, and their fruit never ripens. The seeds that fell in good soil stand for those who hear the message and retain it in a good and obedient heart, and they persist until they bear fruit.

SOME PASSAGES FOR PRAYER DURING THE COMING WEEK

For this week you might pray on the first two chapters of Luke's gospel, beginning with chapter 1, verse 26. You could take one section at a time and fill in the details, imagining what each scene must have been like. See the different people. Meet them. Enjoy the privilege of being there. Listen to them speak — Mary, Joseph, the shepherds, Simeon, Anna. Not just their thoughts but their **feelings** too. For example, you might ask Mary to let you feel some of what she felt, to see with her eyes, to experience some of the 'treasure' she has stored up in her heart. Listen to her describe in her own words what happened. Let her be human. Put yourself in her shoes. Listen to her and let her tell you how she **felt** — for example her feeling of being overcome at how the God of Surprises waited thousands of years and then, out of all the millions of people in the world, chose such an unlikely, unimportant young woman from a country village. Feel what that was like for her — her "Why me, Lord!" — and maybe you'll realise that you too have been specially chosen and blessed because you are not an 'important' person! Listen to Zechariah and Elizabeth tell you of their barrenness, and their lack of hope that they would ever change, and you may recognise your own barrenness and lack of hope. Let Joseph talk to you as a friend and tell you

how confused and shattered he is that the woman he loves is pregnant; then talk to him again after his dream. Remember, as you pray, that what is described is also happening now — you are being invited to say yes to God's entry into your life, you are being given the same privilege as the shepherds, as Simeon, of coming into the presence of the saviour of the world — you may find yourself joining Mary in her song of praise...

If you would like another passage during the week, you could try LUKE 6 17-26 The Beatitudes. You might look at Jesus as he speaks. What do you see and hear him say to you? Talk to him about what he means and what he wants for you. Ask him questions. Or pick out the phrase that means most to you and repeat it slowly, turning it over in your heart and letting it sink in.

You could also read and pray on some of the passages that will be read in church on Sunday.

Remember to take a few minutes to keep a record in a notebook of how your prayer went. Not so much your thoughts or insights as how you felt and what happened for you. Were you able to use your imagination? Did you meet God? Were you real? What stood out for you or surprised you? This writing can be a great help to growing and improving in prayer.

PLANNING

By now you will probably have settled on a place for prayer. If you pray at home, perhaps in a little corner of a room, see if you can find one or two objects that will help to make this place more sacred for you. As well as keeping your Bible there, what symbols might be helpful? — a leaf, a stone, a cross, a seashell, a picture?.. Some reminder of God's glory that speaks to you. Think about it — don't just take the first thing that comes into your head. You want to find something that will assist your prayer. And feel free to add or replace an object as time passes.

Something that I would like to get for my prayer corner is

_____

_____

CHAPTER FIVE: TALKING FROM THE HEART

Not what he expected

At the age of nineteen, Bill had 'discovered' prayer. He had done a course on prayer, and had begun to find new meaning in his life. His prayer was also helping him relate better to his family.

After a number of months, however, his enthusiasm began to fade a little. Prayer became dry and difficult for him, and he began to feel discouraged and disappointed. But he tried to remain faithful to daily prayer with the Bible.

One day, he opened his Bible at the passage he had chosen for prayer. He picked out the only phrase that seemed to mean anything to him — 'My trust is in the name of the Lord.' Slowly he repeated it, over and over, perhaps ten or twelve times. 'Lord,' he said, then, 'I trust in you completely. By myself I can do nothing..' But it all felt like empty words. Bill was tired and disheartened. He felt like giving up.

Tell your feelings

Suddenly, his real feelings broke through, and he spoke from the heart. 'No, it's not true. I don't trust you, Jesus. I have little or no trust in you. I feel hopeless about myself and about my life. I don't like the kind of person I am. I feel like giving up..' And he found bitter tears flowing down his cheeks.

That was an important turning point for him. From that moment, when **he had allowed his real feelings to surface**, when he had allowed himself to talk from the heart, the gospels began to come alive for him in a new and powerful way.

And that leads us into this week's topic. Last week we looked at ways of listening to God. But prayer is a dialogue — talking as well as listening, listening as well as talking. It is important to keep a balance. This week we focus on ways of **talking** to God. As you read the suggestions that follow, however, you mustn't expect them **all** to work for you. Just look for one that helps you. If it doesn't work for you, try another, until you find what suits you personally.

The first suggestion is that, like Bill, you let your real feelings surface, including anger and resentment. Tell God how you feel — 'I am so jealous and envious of Susan that she dresses so well! I hate feeling like this.' or 'Don't ask me to forgive that man. I feel such hatred for him that I don't ever want to forgive him.' or 'It's awful to feel no love for my own daughter, but that's how I am at the moment, Lord.' Or perhaps you are praying for the victims of famine and you feel guilty about how much you have by comparison — why not **tell** God how uncomfortable you feel? Talk about it. These are all examples of **negative** feelings, of course, but sometimes you have to express your negative feelings before the positive feelings — of warmth or affection or gratefulness — can come to the surface.

Obviously, it is also important to express positive feelings too, especially thanks. Indeed, thanks, adoration, sorrow for sin, and asking, are four things that you are encouraged not to neglect in prayer. Some people use the word ACTS to remind them of these four key elements — Adoration, Confessing our sins, Thanksgiving and Supplication. Others include all of these each evening in a kind of review of their day.

Looking back in the evening

The idea is to take anything from five to fifteen minutes before bedtime to look back over the day — many people find it helps to jot this all down on the page of a spiral notebook. You might look back over the various people and events, experiences, thoughts and feelings of the

He felt like giving up

35

An evening prayer

Getting in touch

This whole exercise is quite a powerful one because it helps to ensure that you are being real, talking from the heart, linking your prayer with your daily life. In fact, if your main prayer is in the morning, your thoughts or notes from the previous evening may also be a great starting point for prayer that is more definitely rooted in your daily life.

A beginner in prayer may feel it is too much to try this on top of daily prayer with the gospels, so here is a suggestion. Instead of taking five minutes at the start of prayer to relax and become aware of breathing, etc., you could take that time to get in touch with what has been happening during the day. You would look back over your day in the way that has just been described, or you might take a few minutes to write in a notebook any thoughts, feelings or experiences of the previous twenty-four hours. You could start by saying how you are, and what you are feeling (often you cannot be real in an intimate friendship until you do say how you are). In that way, you become aware of your worries, hopes, pressures, blessings, difficulties, temptations, the people in your life — and you have already begun to talk to God about these important areas even before you open the Bible. Often you may find that the Scripture passage means a lot more to you because you are now in touch with what you need to pray about, or that it now speaks directly about what is happening to you and provides answers to your concerns. Now and again, this kind of 'getting in touch'

day — stopping every now and then to chat with Jesus. Or you may prefer to pick out highlights, like your strongest feelings, or your greatest worry, or the best and worst times of the day, and have a conversation with Jesus about that.

Some of us may have been trained as children to 'examine conscience' at the end of the day by looking for what we did wrong. But beware of that 'guilt trip.' It is important to concentrate mainly on **the ways in which you were loved** — although possibly at the time you may have been totally unaware of God or of being loved at all! Thank God for the many little blessings of the day — someone's smile, your friends, your food, the fun you had at the disco, the song of a bird, the people you met — and don't leave out God's goodness in yourself!

As you look back over your day, talk and listen to Jesus. Say sorry to him. Thank him. Experience his understanding for your weakness. **Ask him for specific things** for the people you met, also for your family, for a problem you need help with. Mention your worries. Ask him questions.

You might end by looking briefly at concrete ways in which you could love your family and friends in the day ahead, not forgetting to ask for help in specific areas of your life. Hear him say "I will be with you. Trust in me. I came that you might be really happy..."

become aware of the storms and fears in your own life

prayer may be so meaningful that you will not even get as far as reading the passage of Scripture.

Your own life and concerns

That is the point of talking from the heart — that we bring our daily lives, experiences and concerns to God, including our concerns about our family and friends, about school, work, money, our marriages, or whatever worries we have at present. It is amazing that many people do not talk to God about the things that worry them most. It is very important that we go to God with our needs, and that we keep praying, praying, praying about that brother we want to bring to Christ, that daughter who is going astray, our work, our marriages, an examination, or whatever we worry about. Unfortunately, many people get so used to praying with set prayers that they talk to God in a completely unnatural way. They may rattle off 'Oh my God, I love you with all my heart and soul' when they might do better to admit 'Lord, I'd like to love you, but I feel very bogged down with all the pressures today. The children are driving me around the bend — or my parents are driving me around the bend! — and I don't seem to be able to **cope** with them, never mind love them. I wish I didn't find fault with them so much... I know in theory that I can't do anything without you, and that with you everything is possible, but I have very little faith in that..'

That is a great starting point for prayer. **It can be difficult to get in touch with God when I do not take the time to get in touch with myself and with what is going on in my own life.** My honesty about what is going on in my life is actually a great help to bringing alive the Scriptures.

The link between your life and the scriptures

For example, a passage like the healing of the man with the demon (Luke 4 31-37) will mean a lot more to people who are in touch with the ways in which they are torn between good and evil, and who are in touch with the confusion and turmoil in themselves that needs to be healed. We mustn't be afraid to express our needs freely — that is part of friendship. Then we can say, 'I am like that blind man, Lord/ or like that leper/ that paralysed man/ that woman who has given up hope of a cure for her bleeding... You can make me well again. Lord, have mercy on me..'

When you pray on a passage like the storm at sea, for example, (Mark 4 35-41), it may help to take a few moments to become aware of what the storms or fears in your own life are. Perhaps a difficult relationship with your father, a teenager, a husband or wife, a brother or sister, a neighbour, an in-law.. Or it may be a worry

I am like Martha

about someone who is ill, or a worry about work. Or an addiction in your life — something that overpowers you. We all have our storms that threaten to destroy us...

Once you are in touch with yourself, you can then take time to meet Jesus. Remember that what is described in the gospels is happening now, and that Jesus is now present, calming your storms, bringing peace into your heart and your relationships. Try any of the suggestions for talking or listening that this course introduces. For example, you might picture the scene in the storm-tossed boat, join the disciples in their fear, and tell Jesus honestly how you feel about the storms in your life. Being honest and real in your prayer can open you up to the graces of his healing and peace.

Becoming one of the characters

Another suggestion is to make yourself one of the characters. When you read a passage, try putting your name into it, 'Karen, do you want to be healed?' or 'Ken, neither will I condemn you.'

Or you could ask: ''Who am I most like?/ who do I most identify with?'' (Beware of identifying with those who are condemned, of course — that is not the good news that Jesus came to bring!) So you may find yourself saying: ''Lord, I am like Martha, busy about many things and missing out on what is most important in life. Help me to be more like her sister Mary.''

The ideal, of course, is to identify with Jesus, so that you may let his power work through you.

But that may be a long way down the road. Your **first** need is to let Jesus call you, look at you, heal you, be your saviour. You must not be afraid to look for that healing or to ask for big things. "Ask and you will receive," he said. He expects you to bring your needs to him. If you identify too quickly with him, you may not experience your need for him and for his love. Whereas, as you keep in touch with him, your mutual love will gradually open you up to letting Jesus work through you.

Keeping in touch

This brings us to one of the most important points in this book — the value of keeping in touch with God throughout the day. The great sin in life is to turn our backs on God, to live our lives independently of God, to live as if God did not exist; to go through our days without acknowledging God, and without accepting the gift of partnership he offers. When you are having a tough time with someone in the family, do you talk to God about it? When you are going through one of those awful depressing days when you do not like who you are, and everything is annoying you, do you talk to God about it? When you are discouraged about being unemployed, or you have a problem at work, or you are finding it hard to study for an exam, or money is tight, or you find you cannot get on with someone, do you turn to God, talking to him, listening to him, telling him how you are feeling? In other words, do you go to God with your neediness, admitting your dependence? (though being dependent does **not** mean waiting around for God to do what he expects you to do for yourself!)

One of the great things about Celtic spirituality was the way people allowed their lives to be filled with God. They acknowledged God in everything. They prayed before a journey, and thanked God at the end of the journey. They prayed their thanks before and after eating. They prayed before they tackled a task or attempted to solve a problem. In modern times, we are losing this sense of partnership with God, and it is something we would do well to rediscover. Catherine of Siena tells us that 'every time and every place is a time and place for prayer.' You can be conscious of the presence of Jesus with you as you walk, cook, wait for the bus, work, shop... That is what this entire book is leading towards — not just one session of prayer in the day, but a whole mentality of regularly tuning in to God during the day, perhaps stopping every hour or so to repeat again a word or phrase of Scripture that struck you at prayer, or to offer a word of thanks or acknowledgement: 'Thank you for the food we have eaten, for the many ways you have loved us today, for my safe journey, for the people you brought into my path. Bless each of my family through the love I show them...'

Different ways

In chapter four we looked at a number of different ways of listening in prayer, and in this chapter we have looked at ways of being more real in how we talk to God. It is useful to have a variety of different methods like these for any passage we pray on. When you have tried one and you feel dry, it may be time to try another. Use a different method of listening, or talk about how you are feeling, or move into the gospel scene yourself, or just sit back and relax and repeat a short prayer. Let the great Potter work on you, for example, as you slowly repeat the phrase 'Melt me, mould me, fill me, pour me...' That perseverance in prayer, instead of giving up when you feel dry, shows a lovely openness to the Father's will — 'not my way, but yours' — and will always bear fruit. In the next chapter we will look at what it means to bear fruit.

let the great potter work on you . . .

SOME TIPS FROM CHAPTER FIVE

Last week we looked at methods of listening better to God. This week we focus on ways of talking to God. Here are some suggestions, but, as before, don't expect them all to work for you — look for one that helps you with a passage. If it doesn't work for you, try another:

● TELL YOUR FEELINGS

Be open and real and let your honest feelings surface. So when you read something in your Bible like "My trust is in the name of the Lord," it may be more real to admit: "Lord, I would like to stop worrying and be able to trust you, but I honestly feel hopeless about myself and my life. I feel as if I'm never going to change!"

● TALK ABOUT YOUR OWN LIFE AND CONCERNS, INCLUDING CONCERNS ABOUT YOUR FRIENDS

Try linking the gospels with your daily life. When praying on a passage like the storm at sea, for example, have a conversation with God about the 'storms' in your own life. A passage like the healing of the man with the demon can put you in touch with the way in which you are torn between good and evil, the confusion in yourself that needs to be healed. Talk about your difficulties, your work, your life-style, your joys and your worries; also your concerns about others, especially those in your own family. Express your needs freely — that is part of friendship.

● THREE IMPORTANT WORDS

Some writers on prayer emphasise three important words — 'thanks', 'sorry' and 'please'. Others use the word ACTS to remind them of the same key elements in prayer — Adoration, Confessing our sins, Thanksgiving and Supplication.

● BECOMING ONE OF THE CHARACTERS

It often helps to make yourself one of the characters. When you read a passage, try putting your name into it, or ask: "Who am I most like?/ who do I most identify with?" So you may find yourself saying: "Lord, I'm like Martha, busy about many things and missing out on what's important in life. Help me to be more like her sister Mary." Another time, you may want to say, "I'm like that paralysed man/ that woman who has given up hope of a cure for her bleeding... You can make me well again. Lord, have mercy on me.. But avoid identifying with those who are condemned — that is not the Good News Jesus brings.

● AN EVENING PRAYER

Take time regularly before bedtime to look back over the various events of the day, talking with Jesus about them. Concentrate mainly on the ways in which God loved you. Talk to him about the people you met, and ask him for **specific** things for them, for your family, and for yourself for the day ahead. Open yourself to letting Jesus transform your life with this simple method..

● GETTING IN TOUCH BEFORE PRAYING

It often helps to take a few minutes at the start of prayer to look back over the previous twenty four hours, or to jot down your thoughts and feelings on paper, or just to talk with Jesus about what happened, about the people you met, or perhaps about your greatest worry now. That can put you in touch with your anxieties, your hopes and joys, your pressures and difficulties, and the people in your life. Many people find this an excellent way into prayer, making prayer more real, and deeply affecting the way they live.

● KEEPING IN TOUCH

The purpose of this book is to help you develop a sense of partnership with God right through the day. That means tuning in regularly to God on the bus, at the kitchen sink, in the doctor's waiting room — keeping in touch with a word of thanks or a friendly acknowledgement, 'Thank you for the food we have eaten, for the many ways you have loved us today, for my safe journey, for the people you brought into my path. Bless each one of them, and bless my family through the love I show them..'

A GOSPEL STORY TO PRAY ON

Before reading this week's Gospel story, ask yourself what the 'storms' are in your own life. What difficult relationships or temptations or addictions threaten to overpower and destroy you? Bring your storm to Jesus, listen to the questions he asks, and let him bring peace and calm to you.

Mark 4 35-41 On the evening of that same day Jesus said to his disciples, "Let us go across to the other side of the lake." So they left the crowd; the disciples got into the boat in which Jesus was already sitting and they took him with them. Other boats were there too. Suddenly a strong wind blew up and the waves began to spill over into the boat, so that it was about to fill with water. Jesus was in the back of the boat, sleeping with his head on a pillow. The disciples woke him up and said, "Teacher, don't you care that we are about to die?" Jesus stood up and commanded the wind, "Be quiet!" and he said to the waves, "Be still!" The wind died down, and there was a great calm. Then Jesus said to his disciples, "Why are you frightened? Have you still no faith?" But they were terribly afraid and said to one another, "Who is this man?" Even the wind and the water obey him!"

SOME OF YOUR COMMENTS

I was brought up to respect 'God's will.' People would have disapproved of you being angry with God or saying anything negative. So I found the story at the beginning of chapter five very consoling. I've often wanted to talk to God like that.

My twelve year old daughter had exploded and said very nasty things to me. I was so hurt with her that I wanted to give her the cold, silent treatment. But after praying about what was happening, I went into her bedroom (she had just gone to bed) and I said 'I need you to know that I'm very hurt, Elaine, but I love you, and its not going to make me love you any the less.' She got up and hugged me warmly. I want more of that kind of prayer!

I had a painter in all week, and the house was upside down. Normally I would have been so upset, but I turned my annoyance into prayer. I never had a clear grasp of the link between prayer and daily living before. I think I'm only learning to pray now for the first time in my life.

I begin prayer each morning by drawing a line through a page and taking five minutes to jot down anything that comes into my head about yesterday (on one side of the page), and about today (on the other side of the line. That gets me in contact with what's been going on in my life and what's coming up. I find it great for linking my prayer and my daily life.

The course is helping me in my Sunday worship.

I like the little bit of practical planning near the end of the prayer. It forces you to come out of the clouds and look at things in your day, and ask yourself what God wants you to do differently. We had been neglecting prayer with the children, for example, and we got started again because of that planning.

I'm getting more out of this than I get out of the scripture study group I belong to.

All the paper was offputting for me at the beginning, but most of us have found the use of the notebook extremely helpful. It's something I plan to continue with.

SUGGESTED PASSAGES FOR NEXT WEEK

There are some suggestions here for praying with each passage, but they are only suggestions. Pray in your own way. It is also suggested that you prepare in advance on Friday or Saturday with at least one of the Scripture passages that will be read in your church on Sunday.

Each day this week, before you start to pray, you might use your notebook for getting in touch with what has been happening for you during the previous day. Remember also to take a minute or two to keep a record in the notebook of how your prayer went. Not so much your thoughts or insights as how you felt and what happened for you. Were you able to use your imagination? Did you meet God? Were you real? What stood out for you or surprised you? This writing can be a great help to growing and improving in prayer.

MARK 4 35-41 **The calming of the storm**. Feel free to return to this story, which can be a powerful one for those who take time before they read to think about the storms and fears in their own lives. You can then turn to Jesus and ask him for his peace and calm.

LUKE 10 38-42 **Martha and Mary**. See a very human Jesus, tired, saddened by all the criticism, needing to talk, relaxing with friends.

See how he always puts people first. Who are you most like in the scene?

LUKE 5 1-11 **Leaving everything, they followed him**. You might try putting yourself into this scene. What is most preventing you from following Jesus in your family life and work? In what way is Jesus asking you to launch out into deep water? You may like to ask Jesus about this and talk with him about it.

Matthew 11 25-30 **Come to me and rest** Tell Jesus what the burdens are that you are carrying. Ask him what he wants you to do about them? Is there a phrase here you would like to repeat slowly until it sinks in more deeply?

LUKE 4 31-37 **The healing of the man with the demon**. In what ways are you also torn between good and evil? Watch Jesus speak and act with authority and power, and go to him with your neediness..

LUKE 11 5-13 **Ask and you will receive**. Jesus expects you to ask for whatever you need, and to keep asking, knowing that your Father wants to answer all your needs. What phrase strikes you in the passage? Why?

PLANNING

What can you do to keep more in touch with God throughout the day? What are the natural breaks in your day when you might become aware of God. What short form of prayer might appeal to you at these times? — thanks, asking, a line of Scripture..

When and how I would like to keep in touch with God during the day:

_____

_____

CHAPTER SIX: A NEW HEART

"What is the point of praying if it doesn't affect the way you treat the children?"

What is the point of your prayer?

John and Yvonne had always been quite religious — it was one of the things that had attracted them to each other in the first place. Each of them tried to make some time every day for prayer. For John it was like a haven to go off to his bedroom after a busy day — a time to look forward to when he could find peace and quiet and relaxation in the presence of God.

If there was a phonecall, however, or if something prevented him from getting this time alone to pray, John tended to become angry and impatient. This was his quiet time. He was not to be disturbed! — did everyone understand that! **Not** to be disturbed!

One evening, the children were in a playful, boisterous mood, excitedly chasing each other up and down the passageway and having great fun. Suddenly there was a roar as the bedroom door burst open and their father came out, fuming at the noise they were creating. His shouting and threatening brought Yvonne to the scene. She saw at once the look of shock and fear in her children's faces and tried to calm things down. But still John ranted and raved. Yvonne got

angry herself then, and they had a heated exchange of words.

"What is the point of praying?" she asked her husband, eventually, "If it doesn't affect the way you treat the children?"

'Me and God'

It was a good question. For it is not uncommon for people to discover the richness of prayer and then make the mistake of 'going to God' at the expense of family relationships. Sometimes we can fool ourselves that we are close to God, but the way we treat others is the acid test — 'By this will everyone know that you are my disciples, if you have love one for another.'

We go to prayer, then, not only to get to know and love Jesus, but also to **follow** him. We are opening ourselves up to the Father's will, to the Holy Spirit forming us into the Body of Christ. Prayer is meant to change the way we live. So it may be important to ask myself how prayer does affect my life, how it affects my growth as a person, the way I spend my time and money, and the way I treat my family and the people I meet.

One criticism of some books on prayer is that they are too otherworldly, too preoccupied with 'me and God,' not encouraging enough of prayer about family relationships, about our work situations, and the practical details of our daily lives. For prayer is to help us, not just to 'love' God, but to love God **and our neighbour**. Some people reading this book will already have experienced one of the many courses now available for improving communication in the home, and it is vital that they continue to work at this communication, for that is at the heart of holiness and wholeness in the family.

The effects of prayer

Now, this love for others should not skip self. St. Irenaeus tells us that 'the glory of God is a person who is fully alive.' Am I more alive as a result of my prayer? Am I growing in self-respect and genuine humility and peace? Am I experiencing the freedom of God's people — from rigid patterned behaviours, from addictions to work, alcohol, sex, television..? Am I living a more balanced life, making time for friends, for nature, for physical exercise, for prayer, for relaxing with hobbies, music, etc.? Surely I have much less to give others if I neglect myself.

This freedom in ourselves can then open us up to loving others. Is prayer having that effect? What respect do we show to one another? How do we listen to one another? How do we talk to

42

and about each other? Is our prayer making us more aware of the needs around us — in our families, in our church, in society at large; is prayer making us more questioning of the structures around us, and more open to responding freshly to the needs we see? Is prayer opening us to building more loving relationships and working for peace and justice at home and beyond our homes?

A practical resolution

But how do we ensure that prayer will lead us in this direction? One way is to link prayer with the concrete details of our daily lives, as suggested in chapter five. That helps to make prayer more effective.

A certain amount of specific planning is also helpful. Vincent de Paul used to say that a judge's prayer needed to be about a judge's temptations — bribery in those days — and

The glory of God is a person who is fully alive

should be directed to those times in the day ahead when he might expect to be tempted. Now, it is not generally a good idea to spend most of our prayer time planning changes. Towards the **end** of a time of prayer, however, many people find it helpful to look ahead and take some time to make a practical resolution. Would it seem reasonable to spend the last **quarter** of our prayer time applying what we have been praying about to your daily life and relationships at work (if we are employed), or at school, or at the club, but perhaps most of all at home? We might ask God how he wants us to express our love and caring for others, especially for those he has entrusted to our care, our own families.

For most of us, our first and principal vocation in life (in addition to caring for ourselves) will be to care for our families. Some people take a different day of the week to pray specially for each of the different members of their family, and, towards the end of their prayer-time, they zone in on that person, talk with Jesus about her, and plan what they might do to show their love for her in the next few hours, or in the next day. Usually, when we ask for specific graces for someone in this way, God's answer to our prayer is something like: "Certainly. I'll be delighted to answer your request, but remember that you yourself are my answer — I will give **you** all you need to love her.' For prayer should be opening us up to letting God's love work through us, to letting the glory of God shine through us.

Glory and praise

And that is the point of this book. Throughout the book, all the communication skills, and the various methods of prayer, are merely helps to us so that our lives can give greater honour and glory to God. For surely the greatest praise and glory we can give to God is the quality of your lives, including the quality of our love for God and our neighbour. Are we not missing the whole point if we make time for praising and thanking God in words, but do not respect ourselves and others — if we continue to be handicapped by guilt or low self-esteem, or unwillingness to forgive, if we fail to make time to chat and listen to members of our own families, to act against our feelings of irritation and hurt with a teenager, a parent, a partner, a brother or sister. For most people, isn't that what taking up the cross to follow Jesus is all about?

This theme runs right through the Bible. We are constantly reminded that God does not want our sacrifices if we are not reconciled with our brothers and sisters. We are told that it is not those who pray and cry 'Lord, Lord' that please God, but those who open themselves up to the

Father's plan for us to love one another. Mere words of praise and love are not enough.

Not as a 'do-gooder'

Now, there is always a danger in emphasising deeds. Some people are compulsive do-gooders — the good they do can flow out of their own needs instead of flowing from a loving heart. There is a tendency in some people to hear the invitation to care for others and immediately to start planning what they are going to do. As we have seen, it is important to make time towards the **end** of prayer for personal planning and resolution. But it is not, in general, a good idea to spend most of our prayer time preoccupied with ourselves, with how we need to change, or with planning what good we are going to do. On the contrary, the emphasis in our prayer needs to be on meeting Jesus, listening as he speaks to us, talking to him, and becoming aware of his love and caring for us and for others. Isn't there something very sad about the nine lepers who were so ready to beg for help but did not take time to become aware of the person who had healed them? — how **could** they be grateful? They did not see Jesus as their friend. When we do see him as a friend, our resolutions tend to flow more naturally out of love. The more I feel loved — and come to like myself — the more I become capable of loving others, as I open yourself up to letting God form a humble and compassionate heart within me.

This is easier said than done. We live in a society which is full of criticism and discouragement and cynicism. We have a tendency to focus on the negative, on what we don't like in ourselves and in others. We have

Glory be to you, Father . . .

been loved and blessed in the most extraordinary ways, but much of the time we cannot even see it. We can find it difficult to count our blessings.

Counting our blessings

And yet, there is probably no decision more worth making than the decision to count our blessings. An appreciative heart is a pearl of great worth. A number of the greatest spiritual writers, who have studied the wisdom of the East and of the West, have come to the conclusion that the secret of true happiness is to focus on the positive. A sense of thankfulness flows from that, and we cannot be genuinely thankful and unhappy at the same time. It is not a matter of **saying** thanks, of course — sometimes, when we are bowled over by goodness, words may fail us, and we may not be able to name the feelings or the sense of happiness and thankful love that can flow over into tears or silent praise, and can inspire us to give of ourselves in return.

How do we focus on the positive like this? Perhaps we can learn from the experience of a young woman named Ruth. For Ruth was in crisis (which can be a powerful time for a change of heart). She felt so badly about herself that she did not think she had any blessings to count. A friend suggested that she spend time looking over her past life, seeing where God had been, and noticing how things had worked out for her, even things which had been painful or had seemed disastrous at the time. He told her to forget about the very recent past because it had been so painful and difficult for her. That exercise had an extraordinary effect. In a few days, Ruth found herself actually admitting that she was one of the luckiest people she knew, and she was able to turn to God with praise and thanks in her heart. Some writers on prayer suggest that those who find it hard to be appreciative might try that exercise occasionally.

There are many other ways of developing a deeper sense of appreciation and thankfulness. In chapter five, we saw the value of taking time to look back over each day and become aware of how we have been loved — and of God's goodness within us — over the previous twenty four hours. When we do this, we may notice a tendency to concentrate on the things we feel guilty about, so we may have to redirect our thoughts to **positive** things. Done regularly, this can be a great help in gradually encouraging an appreciative heart. When we have enjoyed an evening with friends, or a great football game, or a good television programme, do we thank God before we fall asleep?

My soul gives you glory

It is also suggested that we take a minute or so

at the end of our daily prayer time for thanking God — even if the prayer felt dry and dull, or was full of distractions (we saw in chapter one that we should not judge our prayer — in this world we will never know the abundance of graces that God gives us every time we pray). One way to end prayer that many people find helpful is to slowly repeat the prayer of thanks and praise which Mary said in the presence of Elizabeth (actually **saying** thanks often helps us to be more grateful). Better still, perhaps, this modern version of it that expresses so many ideas from Scripture in simple language, and which we reproduce here with permission.

'My soul gives you glory, Lord, and my whole spirit finds its joy in you, my saviour.

For you have blessed me lavishly and make me open and willing.

You shatter my little world, and let me be poor before you.

You take from me all my plans, and give me more than I can ever ask for, or even imagine.

You give me marvellous opportunities, and the ability to be free, and to burst through my boundaries.

You give me the courage to be daring, to trust in you alone, for you show yourself as the ever greater one in my life.

You have taught me that it is by being servant that it becomes possible for me to allow God's Kingdom to break through right here and now at this moment. Amen'

Summing up

We hope that you have found these six chapters on prayer practical, and that, added to the ways of praying you may already be using, it will enable you to **enjoy** prayer with Scripture more. Some dryness and 'desert times' are to be expected in prayer, of course, but one of the reasons why some people have found prayer dull in the past is that they were not sufficiently aware of different methods. When you are familiar with different approaches, you can try imagining the scene, or putting yourself into it, you can talk or you can listen, you can ask questions or tell how you are feeling, you can pick out a word or phrase to pray on — you can even sit back and rest, repeating the same word or brief prayer with every breath. When one method of praying with a passage leaves you dry, you can switch to another. In that way, you will be playing your part and leaving the rest in God's hands. Remember that **it is Jesus who prays in you, night and day, an unceasing prayer of praise and thanks to the Father**. Indeed, one very beautiful prayer is to take St. Paul's line from Ephesians 3, sit back peacefully and repeat a phrase with each breath. Make it a simple prayer of praise to the Trinity as you breathe in and out your praise 'Glory be to you, Father of heaven and earth, our Father, whose power working in us can do infinitely more than we can ever ask for, or even imagine. Glory be to you, Jesus, my friend, my brother, my saviour, whose power working in us can do infinitely more than we can ever ask for, or even imagine. Glory be to you, Holy Spirit of peace and justice and love, whose power working in us can do infinitely more than we can ever ask for, or even imagine.' See how you are transformed and given a new heart as you praise.

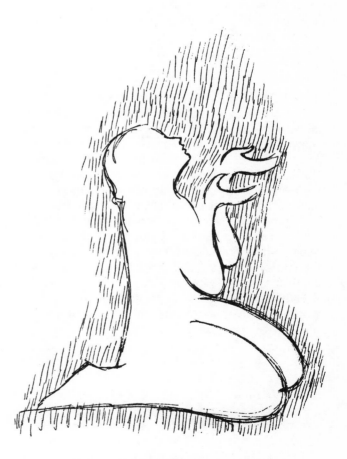

My soul gives you glory, Lord

SOME TIPS FROM CHAPTER SIX

In the first five chapters we looked at methods of communicating in prayer: Preparing for prayer. Calming down to begin with. Noticing God noticing me. Forming a truer picture of God as a loving friend, and of myself as a forgiven sinner. Imagining the scene. Looking at the different characters and listening to what they say to me. Asking myself how the passage applies to me. Repeating a phrase, turning it over and letting the words sink in and come alive for me. In this final session, we look at the effects of prayer in daily life.

1. TIME FOR THANKS

Experts in the spiritual life tell us that the secret of happiness is to be genuinely grateful. Take time regularly at the start of your prayer to become aware of how deeply God loves you, and how much God has done for you, even in the previous twenty-four hours. In that way your praise will flow more naturally from the heart. Many people take time each evening to become aware of how they have been loved during the day. Make some time also at the end of your prayer for thanking God, even if the prayer felt dry and dull or was full of distractions — it is always grace-filled.

2. SHOW YOUR APPRECIATION

The best way to show someone appreciation is not just to **say** words of thanks and praise but to show your appreciation in action. So the best way to give God glory is to live a fuller, more Christ-like life yourself, genuinely respecting yourself and others. Loving others includes making time to chat and listen, to encourage, to act against your feelings of irritation and hurt with a parent, a partner, a brother, a daughter, a neighbour, a friend.. Make some time towards the end of your prayer for a practical resolution about the people in your life, your family, your friends, possibly your fellow students or workmates. Not something for the rest of your life but for the next few hours.

3. HOW MUCH DO YOU PRAY FOR YOUR FAMILY?

For most of us, our principal vocation in life is to love our own family. That gives great honour and glory to God. One practical way is to take a few minutes each day to pray about different members of your family, asking for specific things for them. Some people have a special day of the week for each member of the family. As you pray for and about them, be open to God's answer, which may be something like: "Certainly. I'll be delighted to answer your request, but remember that you yourself are my answer — I will give you all you need to love them."

SOME OF YOUR COMMENTS

I liked the open way everyone talked. I was quite closed to the idea of prayer groups, so this was the first time I ever took part in anything to do with prayer, and I really enjoyed it. I'd have liked more than six nights.

The course has shown me the way to **enjoy** scripture more by wakening up and being more personally involved. I found the Tips great and the sharing of people's experience. Now it's up to me.

I liked that story of the man wanting peace to pray and not seeing the contradiction in the way he was treating his family. I'm often like that. We have one set of rules for God and another set of rules for the way we behave at home.

At least I now understand how my children are being taught to pray. But I don't think I could do this with them... Well, maybe with one of them at a time. But if I tried to do a guided meditation with them, I think they would laugh at me.

My daughter Carol was drifting along, reading awful drivel, watching awful videos, and that was what was forming her mind. I felt hopeless to do anything about these influences, but it never occurred to me to talk to Jesus about my hopelessness. What made the difference was that idea of praying for one person in the family each day. It makes you specific — much better than just generally praying for them all. I've made plans now with Jesus about Carol — I've started having a special supper with her once a week and getting her talking. It's a start.

I appreciated the discipline of fifteen minutes a day to relax and reflect, but I needed the course too. I don't think I could have learnt a fraction of what I did only we had to go through the experience of actually trying out the quietening and praying for ourselves.

I have a sense now of the presence of Jesus in my life. He has given me some of his peace and calm.

A GOSPEL STORY TO PRAY ON

Can you imagine the hopelessness and desperation of the ten 'outcasts' we meet in the story below? Can you appreciate the double gift of healing and freedom that Jesus gave them? And can you see the hope and new life that your faith in Jesus has given you, a sinner who would have been condemned to a life of misery and hopelessness? Open yourself to his gift of a new heart.

LUKE 17 11-19 As Jesus made his way to Jerusalem, he went along the border between Samaria and Galilee. He was going into a village when he was met by ten men suffering from a dreaded skin-disease. They stood at a distance and shouted, "Jesus! Master! Take pity on us!"

Jesus saw them and said to them, "Go and let the priests examine you."

On the way they were made clean. When one of them saw that he was healed, he came back praising God in a loud voice. He threw himself to the ground at Jesus' feet and thanked him. The man was a Samaritan. Jesus said, "There were ten men who were healed; where are the other nine? Why is this foreigner the only one who came back to give thanks to God?" And Jesus said to him, "Get up and go; your faith has made you well."

PASSAGES FOR NEXT WEEK

There are some suggestions here for praying with each passage, but they are only suggestions. Pray in your own way. It is also suggested that you prepare in advance on Friday or Saturday with some of the Scripture passages that will be read in your church on Sunday.

How about jotting down a few notes at the start of prayer this week to get you in touch with what has been happening for you? And remember how helpful it can be to take a minute or two afterwards to keep a record in your notebook of how your prayer went. Not so much your thoughts or insights as how you felt and what happened for you. Were you able to imagine the scene? Did you meet Jesus? Were you real? What stood out for you or surprised you? This writing can be a great help to growing and improving in prayer.

JOHN 21 15-17 **Do you love me**? Make the scene come alive by filling in the details for yourself, the weather at Eastertime, what people were wearing, their faces... You may like to put yourself in Peter's place and let Jesus speak the words to you. How does Jesus ask you to express **your** love?

LUKE 13 6-9 **The barren fig tree**. What word or phrase strikes you in this story. You could talk about the barrenness in your own life or in your family life. Ask Jesus what he thinks is missing — and how you could let him in...

LUKE 10 29-37 **The good Samaritan**. In what ways have you, in your family, been like any of the characters in this story? The kind Samaritan. The two who passed by. The one who was wounded.. Does it strike you that Jesus feels the same compassion for you and has also cared for you as the Samaritan did for the wounded man?

Matthew 14 13-21 **Jesus feeds five thousand**. See the extraordinary things Jesus can do through ordinary people and simple things — but he does ask us to play a small part ourselves. What is he asking you to do?

PLANNING

In planning for the future, what will help you to make time for God in the weeks and months ahead? There are some ideas in chapter seven, but one great help is to have decided on specific short Scripture passages to pray on — even to work through the course again or to take a short section of one Gospel each day, until you have worked right through it. Do you have friends who will support you, especially by sharing their own prayer with you and encouraging you to keep going?

What I would like to do to make time for God in the next few months...

CHAPTER SEVEN: WHERE TO GO FROM HERE

The course on praying with Scripture that Davina had experienced had had a deep effect on her. She felt it had opened up immense possibilities for her life and given her a new sense of direction. She was particularly pleased that she had not been left dependent on others, that she now had the tools to keep on discovering this treasure for herself.

The course had not been organised by her Church, but she had experienced a warm sense of Christian community in the group. One result was that she no longer saw much point in attending her Church service on Sundays. The service now seemed empty and cold by comparison. It no longer met her needs. She would not go back to it.

The friend who had encouraged her to do the course questioned that attitude.

'Your church service is your chief prayer,' her friend said. 'Personal prayer is essential, but secondary. We do not find God as individuals, but as members of this imperfect community into which we have been baptised.'

'Look,' Davina protested, exasperated, 'I went to Church for years and it did nothing for me. I found God as an individual!'

'Did you?' her friend asked, with a smile. 'On your own?'

'Well you know what I mean.' Davina said.

'I do. Maybe the Church is a far cry from what Jesus intended it to be — but turning your back on it is the easy way out. After all, it's your faith-family — a bit like the family you were born into. You don't leave your family because it's messy and imperfect.'

'But I don't accept my family either!' Davina fought back. 'When there's something I don't like, I fight with them to change!'

'And why not with the Church?' asked the friend. 'I believe we have to be very brave in challenging Church structures that no longer meet people's needs. But I still maintain that the public worship in your Church on Sunday is your chief prayer. I believe that there is no such thing as private prayer; only to the extent that you join in the prayer of the whole praying community, to that extent does personal prayer gain its strength, for it is then linked in with the prayer of Christ to the Father. Your thanks, your sorrow, your asking, your daily offering of your life, all gain their strength from that.'

Over a period, Davina did gradually become convinced of her friend's position, and she accepted that she needed the Church.

The importance of a guide

There are a number of things about this story that may be worth thinking about. Not least is the part played by a wise friend. Many writers on prayer point to the importance of having someone to accompany us in our spiritual life. Various names are given to this person — a spiritual director, a mentor, a soul friend. Without an experienced guide, we can easily delude ourselves, or become over-scrupulous, or be driven by guilt or by some obsession. Having such a person to sound off our thoughts against can help us keep a balance. Indeed, having a spiritual guide is probably one of the most powerful aids to our growth in Christ. It is particularly helpful to consult such a person before taking any **radical** step.

The link with your church

A second thing we notice is that the friend helped Davina to see that she needed community, and that an important part of that community was the Church she belonged to. For we belong to one another and to Christ in a special way as a result of our Baptism. It is particularly consoling, when prayer is difficult, to remember that we are not alone, that we are praying with the whole worshipping Church. And it works both ways — people who pray personally will also tend to get much more out of their Sunday worship.

And yet, like Davina, many of us find the congregation in a large church very impersonal. Very often, we **also** feel the need for a smaller and closer community. Indeed, God often speaks to us through others in a group that prays on Scripture together and shares their experience of that prayer with each other. Many people, for example, meet weekly to pray on the Scripture for the following Sunday. This kind of group

the importance of a guide

does not have to become narrowly 'spiritual' — their sharing will probably include sharing on marriage, parenting, or other relationships. Such groups seem to be one reason for the vitality of the Church today in those areas where house groups or basic Christian communities are active. It is well worth praying earnestly for the two great graces of a wise spiritual guide and a small supportive group.

But what else do we need for the journey ahead? Actually, community is only one of the three things that are recommended for bringing alive the power of the Bible. The other two are study and prayer.

The place of study

In the past, study of Scripture was sometimes emphasised at the expense of prayer with Scripture, even for children — but study has a very definite place. What we are talking about here does not require a great deal of education. You might like to read a few of the many simple books that tell about the background to the Bible and put it in its proper context. These include the geography of the Bible and the history and traditions of the Jews, as well as the insights of Scripture scholars. The assistant in a religious bookshop will usually know which books are popular, and the religious section of a public library usually has a few reliable books.

General spiritual reading can also be a great way of nourishing prayer. When first enthusiasm wears off, for example, and prayer may be less consoling, or less of a novelty, spiritual reading can play an important role in helping you to understand what is happening and in continuing to feed you. A short recommended reading list has been included at the end of this book.

dig a well rather than go sight-seeing

Continuing with prayer

Let's look next at the third thing that is recommended for bringing alive the power of the Bible — prayer. Many people commit themselves to daily prayer with the Bible on completing a course like this one. You know best how much time you can make. But it may be important to avoid big commitments which you cannot keep and which may only leave you feeling guilty. Better to promise God five minutes in the morning and five in the evening than to promise half an hour a day and end up feeling guilty because you cannot keep your promise.

You may also find, as you progress, that fifteen minutes is not enough for you. But it is probably not a good idea to extend your prayer time without thought. Certainly not out of a sense of guilt or obligation, but only because you are ready for a longer time of prayer and feel called to it — and provided that that does not interfere with your responsibilities to your family and others.

What to pray on

What Bible passages will you pray on? There are no rules. Some people decide to work right through this course again at their own pace, and they claim they get more out of it the second time. Others decide to begin at the beginning of one of the gospels, say Luke's Gospel, and to pray on one short section at a time, staying with it for a few days, if necessary, but gradually working through the Gospel to the end. That approach will suit some; others prefer to find a passage that speaks directly to them about a present problem or mood or situation. You will find suggestions for suitable passages at the beginning or at the end of some editions of the Bible. A third suggestion is to ask in a religious bookshop for a book with Scripture readings or references for each day of the year. Donal

the place of study

Neary, for example, has a series of delightfully simple books — 'Praying in Advent,' 'Praying at Easter', etc., with a passage of Scripture and a reflection for each day of a season of the year. If you decide, however, to pray on the readings for each day in a daily missal or breviary, it may not be a good idea to take too long a passage, nor to take a number of different passages at a time. Better to take a short passage and to revisit it — to dig a well rather than to go sightseeing. On at least one day each week, it is suggested that you pray on one of the Scripture passages that will be read at your Church service on Sunday.

A word for parents

Many parents doing this course express a concern about prayer with the family. If you feel this concern, bear in mind that you are now actually in a good position for introducing forms of family prayer that are more appealing and meaningful to children of all ages. For your own life of prayer and deepening faith are surely the best guarantee that family prayer will not be mere window-dressing.

But first, a caution. Parents sometimes feel unnecessarily guilty about 'neglecting' family prayer — just because they are not setting aside special times for prayer with the family each day. But it is surely much more important to acknowledge God in the **ordinary** times of the day, pausing for a moment, even in silence, to thank, to offer, to say sorry, to ask a blessing — when we get up in the morning, when we have a meal, when we go on a journey, when we are going to bed... Children pick up more from the general atmosphere of the home than from any special gathering which they sense to be artificial. A bedtime chat about the funny things our relatives used to do, followed by a brief prayer of thanks for the faith they handed on to us, will be something children will enjoy and may remember for a long time.

Similarly, you could sit down with one child to talk about something you are unhappy about — the way she shouts at you, for example (or the way he hits his little brother). Promise yourself you won't argue. Listen to why she shouts and acts like that. What's upsetting her? You'll probably get her talking about problems or worries she has at present. Ask what solutions she can see. Then, when you have finished talking, you might ask her if she has talked to Jesus about the problem, for he said nothing is impossible to God. Encourage her to pray for a minute or so in silence — and pray earnestly for her yourself. Promise to pray more for her. That's family prayer.

If she answers you that she doesn't believe in God (and she may, sooner or later), don't be shocked — that's a normal phase. Encourage her

it is more important to acknowledge God in the ordinary times of the day

to talk more about that. Don't argue, but tell her why **you** believe. And when you pray for her that night before you go to sleep, perhaps feeling a sense of failure, that too is family prayer.

Introducing children to prayer

Parents who pray will naturally want gradually to introduce their children to a deeper friendship with God. Children up to twelve or thirteen can really enjoy stories from a children's Bible, (preferably read to them at bedtime, and also chatted about, perhaps on one evening in the week). The Fount Children's Bible makes particularly good simple, and often gripping, bedtime reading. A brief little prayer rounds off that time before the lights go out.

When you feel ready, you could use some of the methods in this book to introduce a child to prayer with Gospel stories. You might start with just one child — the one who seems most open. Many children **love** guided meditations, but preparation is important. You might switch off the lights, put on some soft instrumental music, and perhaps light a candle (children usually love this change of atmosphere). Try a quietening down exercise like body awareness or breathing, (teenagers particularly appreciate that), and introduce a story from one of the gospels. The entire exercise need only last about five to ten minutes, depending on your children's ages. To get started, a helpful book may be "Guided Meditations for Children" by Jane Reehorst, published by Brown-Roa.

Using gospel passages

How will you introduce the Gospel passage? Well, you might describe the scene briefly in your own words, and ask them to have a silent conversation with Jesus for a few minutes, allowing Jesus to do or say to them what he does or says in the story.

preferably read to them at bedtime and chatted about

On another occasion, you might read a very short passage and ask questions so that the children themselves fill out the details of the scene and then meet Jesus.

Or you might read a passage and ask them to pick out a word or phrase that strikes them, and say why that strikes them — before praying for a minute or two in silence.

Sometimes, instead of a few minutes of silence, you might encourage everyone to share what they would like to ask Jesus for, or say sorry for, or thank God for. They might then make that prayer in their own words.

There are many possibilities, but the best way to discover them is to begin, to try things for yourself. Pray for guidance, and spend a little time preparing to introduce a passage, but don't worry about finding the 'right' way — Jesus is present in Scripture and is pleased to bless our fumbling efforts.

A balanced spirituality

So much for parents, whose spirituality is closely linked with their children. But it may be helpful for all of us to recognise that there are three essential elements in a balanced spirituality. These are summed up in a passage from the prophet Micah:

'This is what Yahweh asks of you, only this: that you act justly, that you love tenderly, that you walk humbly with your God.' (Micah 6 8)

To 'love tenderly' emphasises our relationships with others. To 'walk humbly with our God' emphasises our relationship with God. To 'act justly' calls us to look at how we treat the earth and our environment and its produce, and how we work for justice and peace, making a special option for the poor. In this book, we have concentrated on our relationship with God and with others, but it is important also to be aware of this **justice** dimension for our growth in Christ in the future.

THIS IS WHAT YAHWEH ASKS OF YOU — THAT YOU ACT JUSTLY THAT YOU LOVE TENDERLY THAT YOU WALK HUMBLY WITH YOUR GOD
(micah 6:8)

APPENDIX ONE - A STRUCTURE FOR PRAYER

Below is a brief summary of how a time of prayer might go. Use it in so far as it helps, but don't apply it rigidly. Structures can be useful for helping us to keep our minds on what we are doing, but we must guard against anything that is so structured that it robs us of our freedom and openness to the Spirit.

● MARK YOUR BIBLE — Mark the correct place in your Bible before you start - even read it once at bedtime the night before.

● HAVE A NOTEBOOK AND PEN TO HAND — To write briefly about your prayer afterwards, and possibly to jot down distractions. You might also use a notebook for a few minutes before prayer to get in touch with what has been happening in the previous day - and what you forsee happening in the next 24 hours. This may help to link prayer with daily living.

● CENTRE DOWN — Take a short time to quieten down, to relax your body and breathe more slowly and evenly - so that you will be praying with your body as well as with your mind.

● BECOME AWARE OF GOD'S PRESENCE — 'Notice God noticing you.' Picture Jesus sitting with you, look at a picture, sense his presence, or whatever you find helpful.

● RESPOND — Respond to God's presence, perhaps by kneeling briefly, or raising your hands, offering yourself and your prayer, and opening yourself to the Spirit. Something like: "Dear Lord, I have come to get to know and love you more and to follow you more closely. I haven't come to ask you to do my will, but to open myself to what you want for me. I offer myself and my prayer to you. Please guide me, and teach me to pray."

● READ SLOWLY — Take your time as you read. It often helps to read a Bible passage in a low voice, allowing time for the words to sink in. Stay with any word or phrase that strikes you, repeat it a number of times, turn it over in your mind, meet Jesus, and pray about how it applies to you. Listen, thank, praise, say sorry, ask..

● IMAGINE THE SCENE — Or you may prefer to imagine what the scene must have been like. Put yourself into the scene, listen, and look. Let Jesus do or say to you what he does or says in the story. This is not just imagining - Jesus is really present. Again, 'thanks,' 'sorry,' and 'please' can be useful words as you talk.

● PLAN AHEAD — Towards the end of a time of prayer, look ahead to the next 24 hours - or the next few hours - applying what you have been praying about to how you will spend your time, perhaps especially with your family. Talk and listen to Jesus about this, and ask him to work through you.

● THANK — It helps to end by becoming aware of the fact that you have received many graces during your prayer. Kneeling down with a word of thanks may be a good way to take your leave.

● WRITE — Take a minute or so to write briefly about your prayer. Not so much thoughts or insights as what happened for you, how you felt, whether you met Jesus.. Writing personally can be a powerful way to reflect on what has been happening, and to keep yourself from getting into a rut with prayer.

APPENDIX TWO — A 'NOTEBOOK' PREPARATION

This method of prayer is based on one explained by Bill Hybels in his book 'Too busy not to pray.' Many people find it an excellent and practical way of entering into prayer. It involves taking five minutes or so to 'get in touch' before prayer. The idea is this. You buy a spiral notebook and write on just one page of it each day.

STEP ONE

If you pray in the morning, write 'yesterday' at the top of the page. If you pray in the evening, you could write 'today' instead. Then you take just a few minutes to jot down anything that occurs to you about the previous twenty-four hours — what you worried about, what was uppermost in your thoughts, how you felt about your work, (or your lack of it), about your family , friends, finances, how you prayed, what you did and said, what you enjoyed and what was difficult, what people you met, what blessings you experienced..

There are hundreds of ways of doing this, of course. Some people like to write continuously about whatever occurs to them; others make headings like 'thanks,' 'sorry,' 'please;' or headings as different as 'people' 'God,' 'worries,' 'work,' 'family,' 'feelings,' 'decisions.' Experiment to find what suits you.

The great advantage of this is that it forces you to become aware of how you are living, But don't neglect the positive — become aware of how you have been loved and of how you are loving as well as failing to love, and of how God is active in your life.

STEP TWO

Next, make a prayer — which can be quite short. It is slower to write a prayer than to speak it, but most of us lead such hectic, busy lives that writing may help to slow us down. And slowing down often helps us to listen to God as we write. Either way, this will be a prayer rooted in the experience of daily living, so it will be more likely to flow from the heart.

STEP THREE

Pray the prayer aloud, adding any comments, or pausing to listen to God. It may help to kneel down for this.

STEP FOUR

Now that you have slowed down and got in touch with what is going on in your life, take up your Bible and read whatever passage of Scripture you have chosen for that day, praying on it in any of the ways suggested in this book, but taking time towards the end of your prayer to apply it to one of the areas touched upon in your notebook.

APPENDIX THREE — LOOKING BACK IN THE EVENING

The idea of the evening 'examination' is to take anything from five to fifteen minutes before bedtime to look back over the day — either in your imagination, or, (as in the previous exercise), on the page of a spiral notebook. You might start with getting up in the morning, and look back over the various people and events, experiences, thoughts and feelings of the day — stopping every now and then to chat with Jesus. Or it may be enough just to pick out highlights, like your strongest feelings, or the best and worst times of the day, or your greatest worry, and have a conversation with Jesus about that.

Some of us may have been trained as children to 'examine conscience' at the end of the day by looking for what we did wrong. But beware of that 'guilt trip.' It is important to concentrate mainly on the ways in which you were loved — although possibly at the time you may have been totally unaware of God or of being loved at all! Thank God for the many little blessings of the day — someone's smile, your food, the people you met, the song of a bird — and don't leave out God's goodness in yourself!

As you look back over your day, talk and listen to Jesus. Say sorry to him. Thank him. Experience his understanding for your weakness, Ask him for specific things for the people you met, also for your family, for a problem you need help with. Mention your worries. Ask him questions.

You might end by looking ahead briefly at concrete ways in which you could love your family and friends and those you will meet the following day, not forgetting to ask for help in specific areas of your life. Hear him say ''I will be with you. Trust in me. I came that you might be really happy...''

FURTHER READING

Here are some suggestions for further reading. This is only a small personal selection from the many hundreds of good books that are available.

Neil Boyd **The Hidden Years: A novel about Jesus**. The Hidden Years is a good story, often gripping, written by someone who knows the Holy Land well, knows the customs of the Jews and the atmosphere in which Jesus grew up. But Neil Boyd also has a deep understanding of who Jesus was as he gradually came to maturity before beginning his public ministry. In the book, he is using his imagination, of course, but in such a way that he offers us a unique chance to understand and know Jesus. Published Twenty-third Publications.

Joyce Huggett **Listening to God**. A very good introduction to prayer, written by a woman coming from a Baptist tradition, and telling of her own discovery and reaction to methods similar to those suggested in this handbook. Published Hodder and Stoughton.

Joyce Huggett **Open to God**. You may like to cut out some of the very good pictures from 'Open to God,' frame them, and use them as a help to prayer. You may also like to use her twenty eight meditations on New Testament passages for your own prayer as a follow-up to the present course. Published Hodder and Stoughton.

Gerard Hughes **God of Surprises**. This book, written by a Jesuit priest, comes highly recommended by people from a variety of different denominations. It is about much more than prayer — it is about our journey to God, and is full of good advice and gems of wisdom. Published DLT.

Bill Hybels **Too busy not to pray: slowing down to be with God**. This simply-written book is chock full of common-sense advice and practical guidance. It is one of the best simple guides we have come across. Published Inter-Varsity Press.

Anthony de Mello **Sadhana — A way to God** This is a classic book of prayer exercises which brings together the wisdom of East and West. It is very popular, including with teenagers. A few of the exercises in this course have been adapted from Sadhana with permission. Published Gujarat Sahitya Prakash, Anand, India.

J Neville Ward **The Use of Praying** A thought-provoking book, not so much about how to pray as about prayer itself, what it is, and what it is not. This is heavier reading than the other books recommended on this page, so not for everyone, but worth the effort for those with the patience. Published Epworth.

GROUNDRULES

Those taking part in this programme tend to feel safer when the following groundrules are agreed right from the start.

1. **Take it seriously** — Each person is asked to make a commitment to pray for 15 minutes each day. That is a big commitment, so don't worry if there are days when you are just cannot get fifteen minutes, but the regular practice between sessions is the key to the success of the course. Many people claim that this is the best 'retreat' or course they have ever done, and that it has made them much more contented and peaceful. Isn't that kind of result well worth the effort?

2. **No pressure** — Some people are naturally shy and reluctant to speak, even in a small group. Obviously, the more open you can be, the better, but your privacy will always be respected, and no one at any stage has to talk in the group.

3. **Encourage others to speak** — This groundrule is for the person who tends to talk too much. Please don't speak a second time about any topic until everyone has at least had an opportunity to speak once. Hogging the conversation can spoil the course for others. Please draw others out and encourage them to talk first.

4. **Respect people's confidences** — It is **very** important to respect people's trust and not to talk to anyone else about what you hear in the group. If you say that someone in your family is driving you crazy, for example, that will sound quite different — and may also be hurtful — if it is spoken about outside the group.

5. **Take it slowly** — Don't let yourself get discouraged if you seem to be slow about getting results. Learning to pray takes time and patience, so relax and let God teach you in God's own time.

6. **No preaching** — There is no one way to pray. Different methods work for different people. So please respect people's right to their own approach. What works for you may not work for them. Feel free to say what works for you, but please don't advise others or attempt to convert them to your way. It is important, of course, to try different methods in order to find what does work for you.

SUPPORT FOR PARENTING FROM FAMILY CARING TRUST

THE BASIC PARENTING PROGRAMME

Eight weekly sessions to help parents (at all stages) to improve their communication skills and create a framework of discipline and respect in their families. It is the Trust's most popular programme.

The boxed kit includes 5 cassette tapes, a 25-minute video (for introductory information session) 8 posters (one for each session), a leader's guide, 25 certificates, and one parent's handbook, **'What can a parent do?'**

THE TEEN PARENTING PROGRAMME

Six weekly sessions to reinforce the same skills as the basic parenting programme while dealing with the more difficult situations met in the teen years. Because it is so important to reinforce skills being learnt, it is recommended, but not essential, that parents of teenagers experience the basic programme first.

The kit includes 4 cassette tapes, 6 posters, a leader's guide, and a parent's handbook, **'What can the parent of a teenager do?'**

THE PARENT ASSERTIVENESS PROGRAMME

Seven weekly sessions learning basic assertive skills applied to the workplace or neighbourhood, but especially to family situations. A good way of complementing what has being learnt in the other parenting programmes. Produced in co-operation with Barnardos.

The boxed kit includes a leader's guide, a video cassette, and a participant's handbook, **'Being assertive.'**

THE PARENTING AND SEX PROGRAMME

Five weekly sessions, with emphasis on skills for talking, and getting children talking, about sex - for parents are often overlooked in the sex-education process that targets schools and youth clubs. Preferably for parents of primary school children, but it also looks at areas like dating, television viewing, peer pressure...

The kit consists of a leader's guide and a parent's handbook, **'Parenting and Sex.'**

SUPPORT FOR MARRIAGE

THE MARRIED LISTENING PROGRAMME

Four weekly sessions for groups of married women *without* their husbands, and the results are surprisingly positive - many husbands were so pleased with the *effects* that they then became open to experiencing a course for couples (also provided for in the kit).

The boxed kit includes 2 cassette tapes, 2 leader's guides (one for running single-sex groups, and one for running groups of couples), and a participant's handbook, **'Growing in Love.'**

SUPPORT FOR YOUNG ADULTS

THE YOUNG ADULT ASSERTIVENESS PROGRAMME

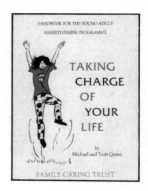

Eight weekly sessions to help young adults, 15-16+, learn the same skills as their parents and thus reinforce change within the family system. The emphasis is on saying 'no' to peer pressure, growth in self-confidence, and finding fairer, less aggressive ways of dealing with problems.

The boxed kit includes a video, leader's guide, pack of 25 certs, and one participant's handbook, **'Taking Charge of your Life.'**

...AND FOR CHURCHES

THE 'PRAYING WITH SCRIPTURE' PROGRAMME

Six weekly sessions, usually as a follow-up to a parenting programme, to introduce people to a variety of ways of praying with scripture so that they can choose what suits them best. There is emphasis on family spirituality. Produced in co-operation with the mainstream Christian churches.

The kit includes a leader's guide and a participant's handbook, **'Enjoy Praying.'**

There is also an *optional* religious dimension included in each of the Trust's programmes.

Almost a fifth of a million parents have experienced these courses to date. In addition to being widely used by social services, and by well over a thousand schools and adult education bodies, the Trust's programmes have been adopted or endorsed by the following organisations:

The Health Visitors' Association
Barnardos
NCH
The Children's Society
Mother's Union Young Families Department
Homestart
All the mainstream Christian Churches - and Scripture Union.
The Psychological Services (Scotland)

Barnardos and the Dept of Health and Social Services have also contributed to the development and production of some of the Trust's programmes, and the basic parenting programme has been translated into Welsh by the Children's Society.